Ancient Wisdom

Elizabeth 'Rainbow Dancer'

BALBOA.
PRESS
A DIVISION OF HAY HOUSE

Balboa Press books may be ordered through booksellers or by contacting:

Balboa Press
A Division of Hay House
1663 Liberty Drive
Bloomington, IN 47403
www.balboapress.com
1-(877) 407-4847

Because of the dynamic nature of the Internet, any Web addresses or links contained in
this book may have changed since publication and may no longer be valid. The views
expressed in this work are solely those of the author and do not necessarily reflect the
views of the publisher, and the publisher hereby disclaims any responsibility for them.

The author of this book does not dispense medical advice or prescribe the use
of any technique as a form of treatment for physical, emotional, or medical
problems without the advice of a physician, either directly or indirectly. The
intent of the author is only to offer information of a general nature to help you
in your quest for emotional and spiritual well-being. In the event you use any
of the information in this book for yourself, which is your constitutional right,
the author and the publisher assume no responsibility for your actions.

Any people depicted in stock imagery provided by Thinkstock are models,
and such images are being used for illustrative purposes only.
Certain stock imagery © Thinkstock.

ISBN: 978-1-4525-0129-1 (sc)
ISBN: 978-1-4525-0131-4 (dj)
ISBN: 978-1-4525-0130-7 (e)

Library of Congress Control Number: 2010917216

Printed in the United States of America

Balboa Press rev. date: 12/16/2010

Elizabeth is a Shaman, a Spiritual Healer; ascribed into the Inca traditions by the the Q'ero Indians of the Andes Mountains of Peru; who has intensely studied with Masters from all over the world and seeks to be perfected by the Ascended Masters from Heaven.

Adopted at the four days old and raised in an Italian family. She had more questions than the priests could answer. Always on a quest to find truth, Elizabeth continued her search. Married to her childhood sweetheart at the age of twenty three, she gave birth to one son. With a continuous strive for knowledge she pursued post education studies in several different areas; Veterinary medicine, Mechanical engineering, Instrumentation, Electrical engineering as well as Welding. She became the first woman Certified welder in all of New England Electric System. It was here where she first broke her back. After ten months of severe pain and many trips to Mass. General Hospital; Doctor Burton explained that surgery would only give her a 50% chance of healing, and in reality, she *could* end up in a wheel chair. Elizabeth and her husband drove home in devastation. In an effort to change the subject, Al gave her a magazine he'd picked up in the waiting room. It happened to be a magazine about Alternative Healing. After an appointment with a woman who studied with the Shamans from Peru; her back pain was gone. In awe, she began intense training into these medicine ways. This was the beginning of life changing transformations. With the quest for healing wisdom and a constant drive to communicate with the "creator who put her here on earth"; Elizabeth continues to strive for knowledge to perfect the wisdom within.

The second time Elizabeth broke her back led her to work with Ascended Masters and Angels. A group of Angels appeared; The Angel ORYON spoke to her: *"Elizabeth, my child; we come to you now with a request of the greatest magnitude. We will guide you to go above and beyond any limitations you have previously held. You have agreed to this venture with us before you were born into this life. You have worked with us in many lifetimes and accomplished significant improvements in the face of humanity. It is now time to help the world move into new states of consciousness. This transformation has already begun a few years ago by those called to the forefront. Many are receiving good information and following through to help Mother Earth. It is now your turn to teach many Lightworkers to remove all boundaries, communicate directly with Spirit and move forward in preparation for the 2012 Ascension. Worry not what others will think, this is your destiny. We will guide you accordingly to recall all of the teachings you have learned in this and all previous lifetimes. You must share all. Trust... it will be fine. This is a new beginning..."*

Although this book was written for Healers, it is beneficial to all of humanity. For the world needs Healers, and needs Healers now. At the time of this writing; throughout the world, there was much fear. For example today's newspaper headlines "U.S. Declares Health Emergency as Cases of Swine Flu Emerge". Now called "N1H1"virus because the term "swine flu" is confusing people into thinking they can catch the virus from an animal. This 'swine flu' is caused by the A (N1H1) virus.

Also in the paper, was a picture of Quarantine officers monitoring travelers with a thermographic device at an arrival gate at Narita International Airport.

Imagine having a temperature, and being quarantined. Now that would really put a glitch in your life. You could actually be plucked out of society and held in quarantine. This book will help you get your own answers. And you will become more independent with your own health to be able to help others to a state of well being. To date, the media is saying a group of college kids vacationing in Mexico are the first to have contacted this virus and brought it back to the States. What concerns me is the mass hysteria and panic that surrounds this subject. You need to be at optimum health and wisdom at all times. Then and only then will you work in a state of competence. Remove all preservatives in your foods and keep everything you eat as close to natural as you can. Stay away from genetically modified foods they will wreak havoc in your body.

When you are spiritually, mentally and emotionally healthy; your physical health will follow.

I dedicate this book to my husband Al; for his unconditional
Love, guidance and support which allowed me follow
my heart's desire and soar with the Eagles.

To my son Marco who continues to impress me
with his natural Wisdom of all that is.

To my father-in-law Barney, who continues
to guide me from Heaven.

And to all of my teachers, on Earth and Beyond; for
without their guidance this book would not be possible.

The magnitude of my gratitude is beyond anything
that could be written on these pages.

I thank you all from the bottom of my heart, with Love, Elizabeth

In order to get the most from this book, energetically as well as intellectually, it is advised to read this book two or more times. The first time, read at your leisure. The second time, make sure to read "Wise Words of Wisdom" Channelings, one at a time with a short moment of silence between each one. Ask the Master of the writing to connect with you and listen for any additional message they may have for you specifically. Pausing at the end of each message will help you energetically digest the vibrations of the Masters words. Digesting and connecting to the Masters will enhance your Spirituality. Spirituality is food for the Soul. Each time we raise our level of Spirituality, our Soul can soar to new heights. Possibilities for Love and Light to come in are endless. Synchronicities of positive happenings begin to unfold on your behalf. Life on Earth can be fun. Life can be our very own creation as we want it to be… Open your mind to new possibilities. Never think or say "I don't believe". Think or say "Show me, Teach me". You will be surprised at the possibilities that come to you and how happy you can be.

This book was written as the Masters spoke to me. I must admit, proof reading in the process of publishing was pretty interesting. It was like reading a book someone else had written. I don't often speak these words in this manner. When I proof-read, it was as if they were someone else's words. Pretty wild because I thought as I typed so much for so long; I'd consciously know each word. These were typed by the fingers at the end of my own hands. I also found upon editing, there were several concepts that were written in many places. My attempt to edit this was stopped. I was emphatically told by Mother Mary, "NO! These words are written here as they should be, in the exact order – and disorder- for a reason." My thoughts were, "it is not proper English here, and not proper grammar there. I was again told, "NO; it is as it should be. Words have vibrations, words at certain times reiterated over again in different paragraphs or chapters are there for specific results, question not, my child; just type!"

Thoughts are things... (before you get into your car, you think about getting in the car) thoughts precede each action and word... Thoughts, Actions and Words are vibrations... Choosing the good ones will keep attracting positive energy of Love and Light to you. This is much more fun and better than rolling with the punches in life's negativity. *Elizabeth*

The Lords' prayer when spoken or sung in the original language of Jesus can raise ones' vibration to the highest levels obtainable on earth today. Blessed Mother Mary

The Lords Prayer in Aramaic with English Translation:

Abwûn - O cosmic Birther, from whom the breath of life comes,
d'bwaschmâja - who fills all realms of sound, light and vibration.
Nethkâdasch schmach - May Your light be experienced in my utmost holiest.
Têtê malkuthach. - Your Heavenly Domain approaches.
Nehwê tzevjânach aikâna d'bwaschmâja af b'arha. - Let Your will come true in the universe *(all that vibrates)* just as on earth *(that is material and dense)*.
Hawvlân lachma d'sûnkanân jaomâna. - Give us wisdom *(understanding, assistance)* for our daily need,
Waschboklân chaubên wachtahên aikâna daf chnân schwoken l'chaijabên. - detach the fetters of faults that bind us, *(karma)* like we let go the guilt of others.
Wela tachlân l'nesjuna - Let us not be lost in superficial things *(materialism, common temptations),*
ela patzân min bischa. - but let us be freed from that what keeps us off from our true purpose.
Metol dilachie malkutha wahaila wateschbuchta l'ahlâm almîn. - From You comes the all-working will, the lively strength to act, the song that beautifies all and renews itself from age to age.
Amên. Sealed in trust, faith and truth.
(I confirm with my entire being)

Contents

Blessed Virgin Mother Mary

The room began to smell like roses, then a dozen, then more. Everywhere I turned I could smell roses. The calmest voice came into my right ear. It was deeper than I had imagined. My intuition knew who it was. Somehow in my dreams I always thought her voice was higher pitched than this. Not so. This voice was deeper, still feminine, yet soothing to the ears. The sound was something I wanted more of. The feeling was so comforting as if I had longed for home for years and finally got there.

The orb began to spin, sort of like heat waves as they rise from a hot tar paved road, as it entered the room. Once it began to materialize my heart began to pound. My brow began to sweat and my breathing intensified. As my heart pounded in my chest; I wondered what lie ahead. Little by little I could hear this voice as if she was sitting right here on my shoulder; yet I still felt her presence with a tingle up my spine. On some level I knew who it was, yet I was scared nun the less. This was my first encounter with full manifestation of the Spirit World. I couldn't help but think 'Why does she come to me?'

The orb spun slower and began to take solid form. Still hearing the voice, I was guided to "breathe, remember to breathe my child; I will not harm you. We come with joy in our hearts to guide you for such project of the greatest magnitude. I am the Blessed Mother Mary" she said.

And here she was, the Blessed Virgin Mother Mary; standing right here in my office. My very first *thought* was "oh no, you must have made a mistake; you want my sister-in-law Annette, she's the Saint in the family. I still swear". Her verbal reply was, "oh yes, I've been meaning to talk with you about that… It's got to stop!" Oh My, Oh My, Oh My! *I said that in my head, and she heard it!* It took 2 hours for my breathing to get back to normal and for me to know I was not hallucinating or having a stroke.

I couldn't take my eyes off her. She grinned as I scanned every inch of her. As a child I wanted details that I never got. I wasn't going to let this opportunity to pass me by without analyzing her. She appeared to be 27 years old. Her skin was perfect, soft like a baby's. She was no taller than me, but she had a slender frame about 5'3". Her hair was much darker than I imagined, it was light ash brown with slight wave to it. Her ears were tiny with perfect lobes. Her eyes were hazel like my mother's because when she turned in the light, at times they were blue, and other times were brown or green. I thought 'why is she always portrayed with blue eyes?' Again she answered aloud, "My eye color is all colors the eye can be; enhanced by the environment" Ah yes! I remember when my mom wore blue, her eyes looked blue. She appeared to me this day wearing a white scarf (it was much thicker than a veil that a bride would but not as thick as her dress or shawl) it draped over her head much like the one that appears in pictures at church. Her dress was light blue, with a white sash tied in the front. The material was made of something I'd never seen here on earth before. It had a soft feeling sort of like fine Egyptian linen that had been washed so many times it had a beautiful transparent sheen. I felt this as she brushed past me; I wanted to touch it and she again heard my thought. "Of course my child", she stated as soon as the thought entered my mind; she held out her arm. She was barefoot and her toes were symmetrical… you know what I'm talking about here, where the big toe is largest, and they range in size from large to tiny… not like some human feet where the big one is the second toe. She seemed to glide when she moved, almost as if she was hovering one inch over the floor. In my amazement I could not tell if she was standing on the floor or not. She was here for real. It was so clear; I was looking at Mother Mary.

Since that day; I can't begin to tell you how many times she moved me out of my comfort zone. I mean, my husband has been raised strict French Catholic. He has a prominent job in society and sports a suit & tie more often than not. Where we come from, people usually end up in the "nut house" when they hear voices.

Can you imagine me telling him, 'honey, I'm talking with Mother Mary'; Gulp! I didn't think it would go over so well. Mother Mary continued: *"This information must get out there and one day your very own son will search for this wisdom. It will be here for him. Write with Love in your heart for your Son. All of humanity will reap the benefits of this mothers' love for her child."*

But wait! I had so many questions. I wanted to know about all those who've passed away, my father, my mother and all of my relatives. I wanted to talk with her about so many things. I wanted to know about UFO's and other Planets. The colonies on mars they're talking about and everything that has been hidden from society. I wanted truth in so many things! She promised me I would have all that information and more when the time was right. She repeated "For now, just type what you hear". Each day I would type, and each evening, I would be rewarded with more information for the many questions I had. I was shown many things in detail and my thirst for wisdom was satisfied day after day.

When I finally relaxed into the realization of the situation; I then wanted to obey. Mother Mary began with "remember those days, so long ago, when you were in Business School? Like a video screen in my eyes I saw me typing, writing short-hand and taking dictation… I answered, "Yes". She replied "Type exactly what you hear. Begin now…" This book is the result of those typed sessions with Mother Mary sitting right here by my side.

This is my first encounter with the passing of Souls up to Heaven: I was raised Catholic and I must admit, I never knew much about the Blessed Mother. Not that I didn't respect her, I only said the "Hail Mary" as part of my daily prayers. In reality I never gave her much thought. Not like some people who have her statue on their front lawn with children kneeling before her. My thing was Jesus. He was my man. I talked to him every day. He was a big part of my life and even at church on Sundays, I'd pray directly to him. God was something bigger than Jesus and something I couldn't touch; never mind imagine. So my connection to Spirit was Jesus.

Growing up, that was it. Pretty much cut in stone; Jesus, Church, Catechism, Prayers. That was my spirituality. I got on my knees and prayed, but I never listened. That was many years ago, so much has changed. I would have never imagined my life would be like this. Obviously, by the way things have played out; I must have agreed to work with Mother Mary. YES; The Blessed Mother Mary came to me one August.

At the request of my friend Phyllis we called to the Ascended Masters to bring us their message for the day. Within seconds my entire body began to shiver. A very loud tone came above my left ear. It was so loud that it was physically painful; I could hardly stand it. Then it felt as if someone had a sledge hammer on my chest, crashing it onto me. Bang! Bang! Bang! My chest crushed with pain. As I began to cry I felt one child after another coming through me. One at a time, I saw each face come into my chest, passing through my heart to my crown and following up to the white light up above me. There were literally so many tears in my eyes; I could not see Phyllis sitting right in front of me. She stayed calm and guided me to stay with it; reminding me to BREATHE. She had me repeat out loud "I am a divine being of Love and Light" over and over again. I could hardly speak as I stuttered the words out loud. She knew what was happening; it was my 'I AM' presence coming into me (waking up), an aspect of Mother Mary.

I had no idea what was happening, I literally thought I was having a stroke! Fear had engulfed me into such a panic I could not control myself. Shaking and tears continued through this process as Phyllis reminded me to breathe.

I realized that every child that had crossed over in the tsunami was passing through me. I stayed with this process and watched them, all traveling up to the White Light of Christ. There were so many faces; infants, toddlers, adolescents, teenagers, so many faces. I couldn't stop crying - it seemed to take hours. Each child was passing through me with a thunderous impact that shook my bones to the core. It was a traumatizing and physically painful experience.

I struggled so much with words to write this incident here to explain what happened. There are really no words on this earth that can give it the credence it truly deserves.

After more hours of meditation and connecting with the Blessed Mother Mary I received answers. She explained to me that the physical pain was due to my fear and ego blocking the process. She also explained that I was Mother Mary in a previous life. She told me that she has reincarnated into many souls in this lifetime. An aspect of her is in many people. It will be my job to find all of these aspects of Mother Mary and help them to integrate as I have. She will guide me accordingly.

Now, each day as I meditate with Mother Mary we pass souls up to heaven without pain. I am just a machine; a clear vessel for them to go directly to the White Light of Christ. Mother Mary told me if my emotions got in the way it would make me physically sick. I still see faces but now I have no emotions involved. It is just as if I was watching someone's slide projector show. I would have never imagined this would be happening to me.

I am so sincerely humbled by this. I thought, oh my, these are some really big shoes to fill. Just as I had that thought, she said to me "you, my child, have already filled them. You have more work to do. Now you must pass the children; past, present and future through your heart to the light. It is your job. This was borderline overwhelming. I say borderline because I don't want it to stop. I am honored to be a part of this and I thank God for making me a part of his world.

Exactly one week after this my experience with Mother Mary, Dr. Ed's father died. Talking with Dr. Ed's wife; I asked when the funeral was. I heard "Sunday at noon; see the guy at the gate and he'll tell you where to go." (Little did I know, the funeral was on Monday) When I arrived at the cemetery there was no one at the gate. After driving around for a half hour I spotted a security guard. He informed me that there were no funerals today, "it must be tomorrow" he said as he drove off in his little golf cart. I immediately knew there was another reason for me to be there. I attempted to drive away; my car was stuck. It just wouldn't go. I stopped to connect up in prayer to see what was going on. At this time I realized I was parked right in front of Dr. Ed's family headstone. There were five small stones representing others that had previously passed. A large hole in the ground covered by planks was obviously prepared for his father's burial. As I prayed I felt the comforting peace and pink light with the smell of roses as Mother Mary came in. We passed Dr. Ed's father as I watched him follow the golden thread up to the sky into the heavens. When I felt it was complete I said thank you and attempted to drive off again.

I was unable to. My car wouldn't move. Once again I connect up to see what on earth was going on again. Mother Mary came into me again. She had me pray to be a pure, clean, clear vessel of Love and Light then we passed souls through my body once again. All of these souls whose bodies were buried here that had been stuck on this third dimensional earth plane. One by one, I saw their faces as they entered my chest. They traveled through my heart, up to my head through my crown to follow the golden thread of the White Light. I watched them as they traveled all the way up to the White light of Christ. I saw babies, toddlers, adolescents, teenagers, adults and elderly people. One man was in a wheel chair, another on crutches, one even had half of her face missing.

I got a feeling of completeness, I held the Light there for an additional ten minutes giving thanks to God for all. As I looked down, I realized my emergency brake was on. Who on earth did this? I certainly did not consciously put the brake on… I was on flat ground.

Al & Aunty Irene were waiting for me at Maria's house. When I walked in, Aunty Irene said "how was the funeral". I said "it's tomorrow". Al yelled from across the room "then where have you been all this time?" (it was now 4pm). I said "doing Prayer." No further questions were asked; it was as if no one even heard me speak. The room was full of people talking, sharing story & jokes. How could I tell where I'd just been & what just occurred? They would think I was nuts.

Having a relationship with Spirit on a daily basis will help make your life to be the best you can be. You become an active participant in and of your life: There is a phrase now which is often written about in new age books; being "A Co-Creator" of life. Now is the time to really know what this means. It's also appropriate now that you learn how to connect to Spirit and get your OWN answers. This book was written for you to take control of your own life so you can stop rolling with the punches and become the Co-Creator of your own Life. Begin to start living your dream now...

There are many ways taught about how to connect to Spirit, some say open your heart. But what does that actually mean. Open your heart? It sounds easy, but when you really think about it, opening your heart is an action sentence which cannot be literally carried out. In reality it is metaphorical. The statement "Open your heart" is intended to feel the Unconditional Love in your heart. And still, how is that accomplished? Think of 'opening your heart' as the amount of emotion you felt the first time you set eyes on that new car; your first puppy or your first mate. Close your eyes and remember the feeling of Unconditional Love you had for your first child. It was a Love like no other. That is the 'Unconditional Love' and how to 'Open your Heart' that we will speak about here. The following is a meditation to help you see, feel or imagine how to connect to Spirit.

This and many other techniques in this book are geared to help you obtain your truth and strengthen your connection to the Divine.

The Great Central Sun

Begin by connecting with that which you believe put you here on earth with Love in your heart. See, feel, or imagine that Creative force which gave spark to your life; whether you believe it is energy, or that which you call God. It is that Source which is known by a thousand names; God, Great Spirit, Creator, Inti Tai te, Wakantanka… When I speak of God I use the words Spirit and God interchangeably because they are *my* names for the energy/being that created me. It matters not what you call this. What does matter is that you believe *this* is what brought you here to earth and that you honor it always.

Once you identify and have a name for that which gave you the breath of life; use your intent to connect with it closing your eyes and sitting in silence for a moment. Think about the brightest White Light that you've ever seen. Maybe you've seen this on TV when someone dies & they're shown traveling up to the brightest White Light. It looks similar to traveling in a tunnel headed towards the Light. Let me explain further… Think about the sun light peeking through the window on a sunny day and how it shows a light stream of tiny dust particles. Picture those dust particles, each one as a golden speck of Light individually vibrating.

Now imagine these tiny gold specks of light floating all around you, there are millions of them floating all around you. Each one is vibrating and moving up and down and all around. As you look up you see the night stars in the dark blue sky. Beyond the stars; on the other side of the Milky-way is that bright Light. The brightest Light you have ever seen. This is the Great Central Sun. (Some call it Heaven; this is where your spark of life came from).

Picture this Bright Light shining down upon you as if a giant was holding a flashlight from up there shining it down to you here on Earth. That Light shining around you if you saw it on a microscope – would look like tiny golden specks of Light vibrating tremendously fast. This is the White Light of Christ. This White Light feeds you as it comes from Creator and pours into every essence of your being from the top of your head sustaining your life force. (The top of your head is called your Crown, and is also known as your Crown Chakra – Chakras will be discussed later in this book). It pours into your Crown and feeds every bit of your energy being.

You can expand this White Light to nurture and protect yourself. With your intent, focus on the White Light coming down from the "Great Central Sun "(sometimes called Heaven); pouring into you, filling every morsel of your being and extending out around you; ten feet in all directions. Like a huge bubble of Light; extend this White Light out the Soles of your feet directly into the center of our Planet (Mother) Earth.

When you bring this white light in and around yourself and extend it into Mother Earth, this is called Grounding. It's like plugging in – as in electricity; you can have all the power plants in the world, yet the light bulb won't turn *on* until you "ground" it. When you "ground" this White Light into the center of Mother Earth and anchor it there, the energy has a constant flow. Feeding you, nurturing you and sustaining you. This White Light is your connection to Source (where you came from and where you will return when your job is done here on Planet Earth). When you connect with the White Light you are connecting to Source (God). When you have a feeling of this energy flowing from the Great Central Sun (Heaven) through you and anchoring it into the center of Mother Earth, at its most intense point; pinch a knuckle on your hand. This will anchor a point for you to call upon it again at any time. The next time you wish to have this energy flow, and you pinch that same point on your knuckle; it will come back to you quickly. Pinching the knuckle is the part I like best, because it helps to recall the energies of Spirit more quickly.

This Connection to the White Light is the Power within you. Honor this and Communicate with it daily. If you wish to get the most out of this meditation and anchor the NLP Point – read this section above and tape it so you can listen to it as you guide the Light through your body, then when it is most intense pinch your knuckle to anchor it.

Catholic

I was raised Catholic because my mother was Catholic, and her parents were Catholic and that's just the way it was. Religion was our connection to God. I learned their many rules, yet there were some I didn't agree with. When I questioned them, I got punished.

How dare I question the laws of God! So as a child I held my questions inside. My inner self was screaming to find Truth yet my physical self was more concerned with obeying my mother. I was taught how to pray but as a child I was *not* taught to listen to what *God* has to say *to* me. I had no idea that Spirit could actually talk to me and I could actually have an interactive relationship with God. Studying with the Shamans taught me how to speak with God; to have Spirit guide my every move. To be able to re-negotiate events and things in my life was as simple as talking with my friend. I believe religions are like languages in so many ways. Very similar ingredients, yet each have their own flavor. Since a child I believed that all religions should be taught in grade school then we could decide which one makes our Spirit soar.

Identify the name which you want to call "God"; then call upon it. It is *that* which you believe put you here on earth. Honor that Source of Creation and Communicate with it every day by speaking *and* listening. Call this Prayer or Meditation; call it whatever you want. Just do it. Some say they don't have time to pray. In reality "you can't afford not to pray". When you sit in prayer, God can make time stand still; so you will never be late for work. It happens all the time. You must have experienced an occasion where you just couldn't believe what was done in that small timeframe; for example driving somewhere, and not remembering how you got there. As if you were teleported from home to that location. Tell God you've only got five minutes for prayer because you must be at work; then pray. It's amazing how much interaction you can have with God's presence during those five minutes.

So how do we know if it is Spirit talking to us or Ego when we pray?

Begin with connecting to the Great Central Sun. See, feel or imagine the White Light on the other side of the Milky-way, then pray. Pray, or talk as if it was your friend sitting next to you and give a moment of silence to listen. During the next three to five seconds will be the answer in truth. After that ego takes over; so in the beginning, keep it short. Ask a question; listen for the answer within those three to five seconds, then be sure to say Thank-You. There will come a time when you will be able to sit and listen to an entire conversation. At first keep the questions simple, short and sweet. Do this at least once a day. The more you do this, the easier it will come.

One of my very first teachers "connected" to get answers. She'd close her eyes; follow her Chakras up to the 8th one above her head then higher and go inside to listen. When I finally learned how to do this it felt like my head was floating. It actually brought you from the Alpha states into the Theta states of consciousness to talk with God. It took years for me to master how to do this particular 'connecting up'. Today it is easy for me to get into that space of quiet with the ability to hear my guidance and my aim is to teach you how to communicate with the Creator that gave you the breath of life.

When you are totally awake and fully conscious, your brain waves are called Beta state of consciousness; brain waves are oscillating between 14 to 30 cycles per second.

Alpha state is when the mind relaxes as in daydreaming or watching a movie (disconnected from the life around you); brain waves oscillate between 8 to 13 cycles per second. Theta state is when the brain waves oscillate between 4 to 7 cycles per second; here is where deep meditation takes place. This is where many can communicate with their higher self/ God. Hemi-Sync© Cd's are available online to help train the brain to reach such relaxing states. Robert Monroe is well known for his research in altered states of consciousness. He also performed numerous documented tests on out of body experiments. He is the founder of the Monroe Institute in Faber, Virginia. Monroe's registered patent Hemi-Sync© is designed to stimulate altered states of consciousness.

One benefit for mastering Theta states of consciousness is creativity and intuition. Delta is less than 4 cycles per second which is a deep deep sleep.

When the right and left brain is balanced one is able to connect up more easily to obtain information. To do this, I sit quietly in prayer, close my eyes and with the lids closed, raise my eyes to the center of my head as if looking out through my crown chakra, then following the golden thread up to the 8th then 9th chakras, until you see the thread of liquid golden light connecting you to the heavens. Follow this thread up until you feel the back of your head floating. When you get this feeling, you may see, hear, or imagine Creator speaking with you. If the information comes in quickly, tell the speaker; (whether it be an Ascended Master or God/Higher Self) to slow it down and speak to you in a language you can understand and a frequency you can hear.

ALTAR

Once you identify your Source of Creation it is best to make an Altar to honor it. An Altar is a place where Spirit can go when you're too busy. An Altar is a place where *you* can go to concentrate. Because it will be designated as your place to pray, it will help you let go of the daily activities and quiet the brain quickly. It does not have to be elaborate with many statues or crosses. It can be as simple as you choose. You can use any items that represent Spirit to you.

With an interactive relationship with Spirit, you walk in alignment with the Universe. Doors will open for you that you never thought possible. Opportunities begin to arise out of nothing; better than you could have ever dreamed. You truly become a Co-Creator of life. When you are filled with the White Light, you are in proper vibrations of Love and Light. Proper vibrations by the "Law of

Attraction" will attract to you more of the same. These higher vibrations draw to you all that you need to maintain a life of Joy and Love.

On my altar I have a Cross with Jesus, A statue of Kateri Tekakwitha and some crystals that have special meaning to me. Kateri was an Indian Saint my mother taught me to pray to as a child; I grew up *believing* she was my Guardian Angel. After my training in Spirituality, I *know* she is. Kateri is First Native American to go through the channels of becoming a saint. She is now Blessed and on the way to becoming canonized in the Catholic Church. It's also nice to write your desires on a piece of paper and place them on your altar for God to manifest. Talk with God as you would your best friend. Be certain you know what you want and be clear with how you want to say it; before you ask/ pray.

Some people don't know exactly what they want. Their words change daily. Until you are certain in what you want, you won't be able to manifest anything. Be sure and be clear in all that you do and say. 'Say what you mean, and mean what you say' and then you will be truly manifesting all you want into your daily life.

My Friend Anne was born in Germany. One day she said, "Deb was here for a visit & when she left, she said; "see you later". I waited all day & she did not return." Anne had a point there. Many of us use words that are not meant in a literal way. When speaking with God, you must mean the words in a literal way, for that is what will manifest. Always remember to Say what you mean and mean what you say. We'll talk more about this later when we speak of the Law of Attraction.

Vibrations

The basis of everything is vibration. Vibration is a measurement of energy of life and it behaves just like magnets where LIKE attracts LIKE. Remember in science class when magnets of opposite poles repelled each other? You couldn't stick them together for anything!

You had to have both of them either North poles or South poles before they would stick together. This is what the 'Law of Attraction' is – attracting to you exactly what you are already vibrating. So if you are vibrating anger, more anger comes to you. If you are vibrating "I'm broke". You'll stay in that state of being broke.

It is law that we are the creators of our own experience. This is accomplished by our thoughts, words and finally actions to carry them out. If we could control our thoughts, then we would attract only those things that we WANT as opposed to those we do not want.

Have you ever heard a friend constantly complaining; you could watch how chaos keeps coming to him. He says his wife is a bitch, his boss is a jerk; even the real estate guy is trying to "screw him". In reality it is his own negative thoughts that are attracting exactly what he does NOT want. Because he is attracting exactly what energy he is already vibrating in. While he complains about everything around him with hate in his words, he actually attracts more negativity (hate/anger/chaos) like a magnet.

In order to manifest anything, you must speak/think in a specific way. The Universe does not acknowledge the word NO or NOT and DON'T. If I was to say to you, "don't think of a purple goat! Now I was walking down the street and not thinking of this purple goat and went to take a turn around the corner and I told the man I really don't want a purple goat and…" Well, what's the first thing that comes to mind? "A purple goat."

The Laws of the Universe are exactly the way things work in the Universe. So as this man says over and over again, exactly what he DOESN'T want to happen, he is telling the Universe to bring him exactly what he *doesn't* want! In his effort to discuss everything negative around him, like a magnet; he attracts more negativity.

Be aware of your thoughts. Thoughts are so very powerful, they precede every thing we say and do! It is our very thoughts, words and emotions when all three are congruent – Whammo! Here it comes! Wouldn't it be much better to think and say exactly what you DO want; and watch those good things coming to you?

One way to raise your vibrations is to focus on the good things in life. Wake up in the morning, saying, what a great beautiful sunny day it is. Notice you must keep the words in the present tense and not the future by stating "it will be a sunny day". If the words are in the future, that sunny day will be like a carrot dangling in front of you never coming to fruition. Find good things to think and talk about. They must be true statements in order for this to work. Choose statements that will encourage you and lift your spirits. Some statements for encouragement are: I love the beautiful sunshine, I am grateful for the birds singing this morning, I enjoy this delicious cup of coffee, etc… find things that are absolute and enjoyable. If you look around you, there are many little things that you could find. Being grateful will most eloquently raise your vibrations and enhance your emotions.

To quote Ester and Jerry Hicks in their book *Money and the Law of Attraction*; "You do not have to understand electricity to be able to turn on the light, and you do not have to understand vibrations in order to feel the difference between harmony and discord".

How do we know when we are out of alignment? When we begin to get obstacles in our way. One day I was to drive to a class in upstate NY. It was a five hour drive. With the car packed I was backing out of the driveway & remembered that I forgot to unplug the coffee pot. I ran back in the house to unplug it, leaving my keys on the counter. Once again in the car, I could not find my keys. Returning again into the house I saw them on the counter & realized I had not fed the bird. After feeding the bird I ran to the bathroom and the phone rang. This was one hour after my initial backing out of the driveway; on the phone was the woman canceling the class in NY because of an emergency. Had I not been interrupted so many times I would have been well on my way and wasted all that gas. When obstacles come to you, think about them. Maybe they're telling you to 'take another path' or to 'so something else'. Obstacles come in many forms, take note when they come for they are surely trying to tell you that you are headed in the wrong direction; sometimes literally; sometimes metaphorically. Metaphorically as in - maybe you shouldn't be working with that teacher/ dating that person? Stop and think. Sit a while and ask God for more specific guidance to be clear… then see/feel or imagine the answer. The more you do it, the clearer the messages will be.

We all have a guidance system in our bodies; it is how we feel. When we feel good, we're doing the right thing; (unless you are under some sort of influence such as alcohol or recreational drugs). When 'something's a miss' stop & take notice. Your guidance system is trying to tell you something. Take notice of the animals/ nature and birds around you and think about the messages they have for you.

I've connected with animals since I was a child; I can remember staring out the window when I was at school, wishing I could play with the squirrels. When I began to drive on the highway a Raven coming close to my windshield would always precede a police officer hiding around the bend. Occasionally it looked like the bird was going to hit my window. I began to interpret the signals the birds had for me. Depending on what a hawk is doing will tell me there is trouble up ahead. Each person's interpretations are unique to themselves. Today I may find my meaning for Hawk to be "words can slash you like the talons of the hawk" (be alert for others' words) and tomorrow I may need to be keen and alert on the road, when I see a Hawk. Animals and Nature talk with us; we just have to learn to understand their language; be patient, they will teach you. Animal Speak is a book by Ted Andrews. This book can help you be familiar with animals and their messages. It's a fun book with many great ideas. For Example: when you read about the Fox, one sentence or a few words will jump out at you having more meaning than the rest… That will be your message for the today. Another day reading the same pages about the fox; different words will stand out for the message of that day.

The Deer have been coming to our back yard since we moved to the hill in 1987. Last May the one I call Tumaguy (female) came with two babies. Scratch (another female that has a white mark on her nose) also came with two babies and Lil' ONE (another tiny female) came with one baby. Yes, in May of 2008, five babies were born right here in our woods. I feel so blessed to have these beauties right here. They come every day at dusk and dawn. I am doubly blessed because it is illegal to hunt this side of the highway in our town so these beautiful animals will be with me for a very long time.

Eight years ago when I first spotted Tumaguy; I gave her that name because she had a baseball size tumor on her right shoulder. She was not laboring in any way and came twice a day with a family of deer. Sometimes nine sometimes fifteen, one day she came with twenty-four deer of all sizes. In my connection with these deer I began to wonder what the symbol of the tumor meant to me. In meditation I was guided to make an appointment with my Doctor for a check up. I had a tumor on my back. As soon as my tumor was taken care of, Tumaguy's tumor burst and never returned.

Some healers think the animal is taking the health issue away from you. I've found this is not the case. You still have to deal with the issue yourself. The animal is only showing you what is there. When your cat has dental problems, be sure to have your teeth checked. When your dog has diarrhea, watch what you're eating.

Nature speaks in so many ways. My buddy Mr. Mitchell taught me that when the leaves on the trees turn upside down, it means we're headed for a big storm. When the squirrel's tails are thick and bushy, it is going to be a long cold winter. Pay attention and take note. Soon things will make sense and the picture will be clear.

Interact with Spirit everyday, everywhere. Pray over your food and give thanks for it giving its life for you to live. Send a prayer to the ambulance driving by. Send a prayer for your family and friends. Remember to give thanks often. Practice integrity. Live in a place of truth without judgment. Then take action with your prayers.

Begin to put them into motion. God is not going to bring that new house to us while you sleep. We've got to meet him half way. God will bring us opportunities, but we have to take them and put them into action.

Walk in nature connect with the trees, birds and squirrels. Watch the way they interact with nature. Listen to mother earth and hear her heartbeat. Listen to the voices of the animals. They can teach us so much about Unconditional Love. Imagine the connection we have to all of life. The breath within each one of us lets us know we are truly all connected. You may have just felt goose-bumps when you read that statement. When you hear truth, often, it will bring chills up and down your spine. I call these truth bumps. When it is enormous truth you may even feel these bumps all over your body. You will have no doubt of what I'm speaking about here, when you feel it you'll know it; it's intense, like nothing you've ever felt before.

This oneness people speak of today is our connection to all. The picture of life is bigger than we know. Actually God is us and we are God. We are truly One with ALL that is, ONE with God. It is in this oneness that miracles occur. There are groups now on the internet that gather together for prayer for peace for the entire world. It's been scientifically proven that there is less crime during such time. I love it when science proves the power of prayer. Dr. Masaru Emoto has published several volumes of work titled "messages from water"; showing that prayer/ positive intention said over water actually changed the molecules. Many Prayer and intention experiments are available on the internet all you have to do is search.

There are a lot of different energies in the world today. Whether you are a Healer and take on others' pain or working in a retail job. There are so many forms of Heavy Energy. Jealousy, fear, worry, depression and anger are only a few to mention. It comes from many places such as world events, clients, family, friends and even our pets.

The Aura is your subtle (invisible to most) energy field that extends beyond your physical body. Often Aura's extend six inches around the body some are twelve to eighteen inches and rarely some exceed ten feet. There are many layers and corresponding colors and vibrations pertaining to your whole being; in your energy field/ Aura. Your Chakras and Meridians (also invisible to most people) run through this field connecting your physical body, mind, spirit and emotions. Meridian lines run through your body like a map of your electrical system connecting all of your organs and moving freely when you are healthy. When there is dis-ease, a meridian line will block/ kink and reveal stagnant energy. Constructive energy work can be performed in the Aura with the Chakras and Meridian lines to move stagnation and keep you healthy and stress free. I have friends who are Shiatsu' practitioners and acupuncturists who are experts in this area; their sessions are extraordinary. Be sure to interview the practitioner before letting him/her work in your energy field and on your body. When on the table in the practitioners office, you are vulnerable and open. Be sure you are working with a person of high integrity. Check with your higher guidance before working with this close with anyone.

Protection is a defense screen around the Aura that safeguards your inner and outer being. You create 'protection' to safeguard yourself from unwanted heavy energies. There are many different forms of protection as there are belief systems. Once you decide which you will use, along with Prayer; then trust that it be done. Protection will help balance and calm your emotions, eliminate obsessive thoughts and reduce stress; allowing joy, love and harmony back into your life so you can focus on the task at hand.

Ask yourself these questions:

Does watching the news leave you feeling upset or drained?

Do family, friends, partners, or even your own thoughts leave you feeling exhausted?

Are you unable to stop thinking about that argument you had with someone? (tape-loops)

Does commuting to and from work leave you worn out?

Is your mind racing about what you did or have to do; preventing you from a good night's sleep?

Has the energy changed when someone came to visit?

Do you have a new ache or pain that wasn't there before; and you've done nothing to cause it?

Is someone jealous of you or talking about you in unhealthy ways?

Do you habitually drink alcohol the same times each week? or each day?

Do you smoke marijuana ?

Are you having negative thoughts?

Do you Anger easily?

Are you having "bad luck"?

If you answered yes to any of these questions you may need Protection from heavy energies. Even jealousy from another person or smoking marijuana can put holes in your Aura; cutting it like a knife. You may feel exhausted for no reason at all.

First and foremost, no matter which protection you decide to call upon and build, it is crucial to call in the White Light. This is an absolute. Remember this always.

After reading that last section I realize there are some of you who think, oh, not me. Marajuana helps me get into altered states quicker, easier. This section is for you.

If you had the direct phone number to God, and it was 8888, would you dial 666 and wonder why God's message was not there???? The rules are simple. These techniques have been tried and tested for 14 years (I've witnessed others try to alter things here and watched as they spun in chaos day after day). Altering these techniques doesn't work. The methods in this book are what work for me, accurate and truth. If you think you can have a glass of wine and get accurate answers, try it. When it doesn't work, resort to the beginning of this book and start reading over again. Of course, that is, if you really want to find truth and guidance from Source/ the Creator God who gave you the spark of life.

The following are several different types of Protection:

1) **Bubble of Protection**

Connect with God and call in the White Light of Christ; balance this White Light by focusing it into your Crown Chakra (head) and spreading it throughout every morsel of your body, grounding it into Mother Earth just as discussed earlier in this book. Push this White Light around you ten feet in all directions. This is the White Light of Christ Bubble. Nothing dark, negative or evil can enter or penetrate through when you are filled with the White Light of Christ. To insure it is a solid bubble of protection we must be impeccable with our actions. You can not go around cursing or talking about someone else and think this bubble is solid. Cursing, gossip and basically being irresponsible will put holes in this bubble. You must take responsibility for your actions. Smoking Pot, alcohol and recreational drugs are other ways to put holes in your Aura as well as easily destroy any protection you've built. Take control of your life and strive for integrity. This will be the most solid foundation of any protection. When you encircle yourself in the White Light of Christ, keep it strong, bright and connected to the Great Central Sun along with Mother Earth at all times. You should feel this energy flow through you and around you. It will be like a solid bubble – repelling off the negative/ heavy energy of the world. Practicing unconditional Love for all and giving thanks often as well as doing good deeds (without conditions) will strengthen it. Negative energies hate the light; bring in the light!

When you fill yourself with the White Light of Christ (aka White Light), you become illuminated. When you are fully illuminated, nothing dark, negative or evil can enter or penetrate through. For Darkness cannot exist in the Light. Be vigilant and fill yourself with Light every day.

If I were to paint a visual picture for you of the White Light of Christ Bubble, as it came from the Heavens shining down upon you circling you it would look like a giant piece of bubble gum where you blew the perfect bubble and you stepped into it as it was still connected to Heaven and Earth.

2) Archangel Michael

Archangel Michael is the Archangel of protection.

Connect with God and fill every bit of yourself with the White Light of Christ. Call upon Archangel Michael and ask him to use his sword of blue flame. Explain to him what is going on and how you are feeling. Use all of your senses in describing what's happened. Tell him what you see, hear, feel and imagine. Speak to him as if you are sitting right next to him. He can hear you. Give him details so he can help combat them. You can call upon him at any time and as often as you like. He works for you but cannot come to help you unless you call him. That is the law of all the Archangels; they cannot intervene until they are asked. Once you call him, trust and

23

know that he will come to combat any heavy energy in and around you. You may even begin to see blue lines in your field of vision as you move your eyes around the room.

3) The Violet Flame of St. Germain

Basically St. Germain works in the same way as the Archangels, he needs to be asked before he can help us. Sit in a quiet, and call upon St. Germain. See, feel, imagine and allow your thoughts to flow to St. Germain. Ask him to surround you with his violet flame of transmutation. Any thing that comes into contact with this flame will be instantly transmitted to the Heavens for healing and transformation. What this means is that the heavy energy hits this flame, and it is instantaneously sent up to Heaven where God changes the Heavy Energy into Love and Light to rain back upon Earth in a healthy way. This violet blue flame is just like the welders torch. When the perfect mix of oxygen and acetylene (gas) are reached you get the perfect bluish/ violet color. If a solid passes through this flame it becomes a liquid. If a liquid passes through this flame it becomes a gas. Nothing can pass through this flame without changing state. Call upon St. Germain at any time you need assistance and he will provide.

4) Sage

Using your intent; with prayer. This means to intend to clear any and all negativity, including but not limited to anything dark, negative, evil, any demons or entities of any kind, poltergeists, curses and any negative spiritual influence. Negative energy can be as slight as bad word spoken about you, to severe, as someone wishing you dead. All of these are classified as Negative/ Heavy Energies. Sage is meant to be a **Ceremony** more than a Literal way of moving the smoke into every corner for cleansing. Sage can be used to clean your home, business or surrounding area from heavy energy. You can purchase a bundle of sage for under $11.00. In addition to Sage you will need a six inch feather, a lighter and a huge ashtray to catch the hot ashes as the sage burns. Light the sage and quickly blow it out so you're left with a light smoke. With the feather, fan the smoke into every corner of the house, basement, attic and closets. Walk throughout the entire home with the intent to cleanse and remove any heavy energy, and replace it with Love and Light. You must be conscious at all times of the hot ashes and where they fall. Hot ashes will burn and may ignite to fire. Keep away from combustibles and children. Anytime you wish to cleanse or protect an area, you *must* have permission from the owner.

5) Sea Salt Baths

Sea Salt Baths are very cleansing and great for removing stress. Fill the tub with four cups of pure organic sea salt while filling it with warm water. Always test the water with your toes before stepping in. Step into the tub and relax into the beautiful warmth with the intent to release anything that does not serve your highest good. If possible hold your nose & quickly wet your hair three times. This will make sure the sea salts have touched every bit of you. Sea Salts are extremely purifying. Stay as long as you wish; yet make sure you exit the water before it gets cold. It is best to take this bath before bed so you can sleep without rinsing off. The sea salt minerals will actually feed your hair and make it silky. When you shower and rinse off the next morning you will free energized and refreshed.

Sleep with your head facing East or North for a better night's sleep. The earth energies run in a North/South and East/West direction… Try this if you are not getting a good night's rest.

6) Florida Water

Florida Water is men's cologne from Peru. The Shamans in Peru use this spray to summon the Good Spirits/ God. They believe sweetness is what honors Spirit; it has been used for centuries. To program the spray: Put the Florida Water in a mist bottle and say a prayer over the bottle for God to make this spray cleanse and purify your space, sending any heavy energy up to the Light for healing and transmutation. For God to bring back healthy, positive energy of Love and Light with the spray of the mist. Then spray this around yourself or your home, you can do this as often as you need. Do NOT spray into your eyes, nose or face. Keep away from babies, flammables and pets. After programming Florida water with Prayer it can be used as Holy Water.

There are also many 'cleansing sprays' on the market today. Check your source. Make sure they manufactured this spray with Integrity; Love & Light. Program it with prayer the same way as you would Florida Water.

7) Meditation

I found that meditation can be done in many ways. Don't get upset if you cannot hold a Zen meditation perfectly as stated in text books. Those can be difficult. All you really need to do here is to find some quiet time for yourself and sit in Prayer. Sitting quietly listening is just that; 'meditating'. Connect with God. Call in the White Light and hold that vision and relax. It's most important that you relax & just 'Be'. If you still have chatter going on in your mind it may help to repeat sounds such as OHM, or listen to tones, or music of monks chanting. Repetitive sounds and words will help clear mind chatter. It is your emotions and thoughts being relaxed in prayers that will keep emotional vampires away. Do this meditation as many times as you need to and for as much as you need in the beginning. Once you have a feeling of how to get into that relaxed state in prayer, you will only need two minutes to remove the stresses and accomplish the clearing & protection required. The goal here is to get to that 'quiet place in your mind any where, at any time; no matter how many people are around you. You'll get to the point where you can find your quiet place in your mind at a rock n' roll concert if you needed to.

You can also strengthen your Aura by Staring at a candle for ten minutes a day for thirty days. If you can do this fine; it's *not* necessary to take you to your quiet place in your mind or to get your answers.

8) Music

Play Music – Spiritual Music, hymns, nursery rhymes, Christmas Carols, Classical Music. Playing music will fill you and your home with Love and Light. Stay away from sad songs with lyrics that could bring you down, talk about hate, murder, anger or jealousy. Of course play them at a nice volume; blasting the music so loud your neighbors can hear will surely defeat the purpose of harmony, Love and Light. Not everyone likes the same music as you do or wants to hear it at the same time that you do. Be courteous and conscious of your actions at all times.

Integrity and impeccability strengthen the Mind, Body and Soul. You are only vulnerable in those places where fear lives within you. Fear is the absence of Love. Did you realize that when you have fear – you are attracting exactly more of that FEAR to you? Fear is a lower form of vibration and because of the *"Law of Attraction", remember that which you vibrate in, will be attracted to you. Remove Fear at once by asking where this fear is coming from? When you get into a state of curiosity you will actually be moving your vibration up a notch and out of fear.

Remember we are never a victim. Take responsibility for everything that happens to you. Remember you choose this world and only YOU can change it. Any of your choices for Protection will work *until* you do something to attract Heavy Energy again. So it is wise to be very aware of your own stuff; because we can attract heavy energy by our thoughts, words, emotions and actions. Your safety depends upon your alignment with God.

In the morning when you stop to get a coffee on the way to work, the girl hands you your cup of Joe, with your change. You have choices; you can smile and say 'keep the change'. Or you can bitch to her about how she gave you the wrong one yesterday... I call this the ripple effect. If you say Thank You with a smile and kind words; then she will in turn smile to the guy after you, and he will go to work and make someone else happy. I've since heard of the phrase "pay it forward". This is a new concept where someone at the market, or Dunkin donuts Coffee shop, will give his change for the next person in behind him. This is on the same lines as the ripple effect. You have choices. Choose happy ones. When you become the change you want to see in the world. It will come back to you ten fold.

Connecting with Spirit Guides

There are as many Spirit Guides as you can imagine. Spirit Guides come in many forms. Angels, Saints, Ascended Masters, Souls who have incarnated on this planet; and some who have never been here before can also be Spirit Guides. At times these Guides will contact us. Other times we may have an interest in contacting them. Above and beyond all, command to only work with Guides of the White Light. These are the ones who work directly for God. Demand all others go to a place that can do no harm, and refuse to work with them, until you are proficient enough to send them to the Light. It is imperative to work with the White Light and ONLY the White Light guides. I cannot stress this enough. Other forms and entities will wreak havoc in your lives, can be very dangerous, and life threatening. If you feel inquisitive to deal with dark forces, you should seek help with a Master Shaman who works only with the LIGHT. This is not something to play with and can be life threatening.

As a child my mother told me I was born in a mushroom basked and given to her by the Indians. She said I came from Kateri Tekakwitha. Kateri was the first Native American to be Blessed by the Catholic Church. Mom was twenty-three years old on her death bed with pork poison (trichinosis). She was at a hospital in upstate NY. A priest came to give her the last rites left her with a card of Saint Kateri. Mom made it through that sickness and lived for many years after that, but unable to bare children. The mushroom basket was her answer to my Adoption and how I was gifted to her. So it was fitting for me to talk with Kateri the first time I tried to connect with a Spirit Guide.

I sat in prayer just like we spoke of in the beginning of the book. Connecting with the White Light of Christ and calling in this White Light from the Great Central Sun, directing it to my head and focusing it through me, spreading it out all around me, down through my feet and anchoring it into the center of mother earth. It was at this time I could *picture* it coming out my feet. I saw myself rising up upon the earth, as I stood standing on the state of RI, and as I rose higher, I saw myself standing on the USA, and then I saw this light coming right out the souls of my feet going in through the earth, and hooking right around the place of the equator, only *deeper* right into the middle of the planet! The light coming out my feet had a pinkish hue. When I asked Kateri what this pink color was, she explained it was the "Unconditional Love" which anchors us to the Earth. This Unconditional love she spoke about was "like the love one has for a puppy or a new born child". This is in actuality Love without conditions. Love, Truth and Non-judgment are actually the gateway between the worlds.

The veil between this world and the next is very thin. Although it can be invisible to most, some can feel it, and some just know it exists. All you have to do is go in prayer and ask for that Guide to come to you. Then open your heart and wait. One of your senses will pick up something while you wait. You may begin to smell something, a fragrance not present before. When the Blessed Mother Mary comes, she is often preceded by the scent of roses; sometimes so strong it is as if the room was filled with hundreds of long stem roses.

Kateri always comes to me with a sweet scent; like a floral perfume. The first time I contacted My Grandfather; I smelled the scent of moth balls. It was so strong and nasty.

Instantaneously I thought "why moth balls"? I was shown a picture of his sweater vests with the little pockets. I knew right away - the fact that for years my aunt would argue with him for hiding moth balls in those pockets. (he was afraid moths would eat his woolen sweater). Now when I get that scent, I smile, because I know my grandfather is nearby. Spirit Guides and God will speak to you in the way that is best for you to understand.

For me to get a smell before a vision was so appropriate to my personality. Each time I was in a panic, that sweet smell would appear. At the birth of my child and every surgery I had was preceded by the sweet smell of perfume. Once I identified it was Kateri, I was at ease knowing I was safe and all would be fine.

If you get a smell first don't get discouraged, you will eventually build upon all of your senses. Some people get a "feeling". Some even get the information as if it were a scene in a movie with the landscape, people and events taking place. Soon you will be able to "see" as well as "hear". At first it may seem as though you catch something in the corner of your eye, then when you turn to focus on it, it disappears. If you could practice looking at things in your peripheral vision you will soon begin to see shapes and forms. Tones we hear in our ears can be followed as if a thread was connected to the sound. Practice following the sound and see, feel or imagine where it takes you. When you have an idea and it seems to come from "out of nowhere". That is usually a sign that it comes from Spirit. When it is so surprising and not even in your consciousness to dream it that way... That is another way we know it is coming from Spirit or our Spirit Guides. When working with God and Spirit Guides, they will NEVER tell you to harm yourself or any other person or animal. If anything like that ever comes in, refuse to communicate with that being; it is not of the Light.

One time when I was talking with God, I heard the answer 'follow the earthly measures'. I absolutely knew this statement was coming from Spirit – because I would *never* use those words together. In fact I can not even say them today; my tongue seems to get tangled in my teeth! Absolutely refuse to work with anything less than the White Light of Christ. As long as you are in Prayer and as long as you work with only beings of Light; your guidance will come from Spirit for your highest good.

Practice, Practice, Practice makes perfect. Go through the steps each and every day, even if you do not receive answers at first. One day it will come. Pray every day and give a few minutes for Spirit and

Spirit Guides to speak to you. One day, when you least expect it, you will get the information you are seeking.

You may have heard of the phrase "let go & let God". What this means is to put your prayers out there, and just wait. Do not have an attachment to the outcome (or it will take forever). Think about this for a moment. It's the same as when you order a new couch from the furniture store. You pick it out, pay for it, schedule a delivery date, then go home and continue living your life. You pick the kids up at soccer practice, do the shopping; prepare dinner - forgetting about the couch you just ordered. You wouldn't call the store every minute saying "where's my couch?"

Manifesting is the same way. When you need something to happen; put your prayers out there, trusting that God will bring them to you. When you question "why hasn't it happened yet"? You are interfering in what God can do for you. When you pray and give so *many specific details* about what you want to happen, you limit what God can do for you. Put your prayers out there with a dream, a vision, a beautiful emotion, and then "Let go & Let God" bring it to you. Trust that "Thy will be done". When you know what you want and your thoughts, words and emotions are congruent then and only then will it come to fruition.

The Akashic Records are the records of everything that ever was and will be; kept in the library in Heaven. In prayer some connect with the Ascended Masters to request permission to view these records. Once you receive permission, you may see, (as if reading them in a book) feel (as if an idea) or hear someone telling you the information.

One Prayer commonly used to contact the Akashic Records is: "I ask God to have the Shield of Love and Truth around me permanently so only God's Love and Truth exist between me and you. I allow the Masters and Teachers of me to speak to me to say whatever they wish". You can say this prayer before you connect with the Ascended Masters and ask them to take you to the Akashic Records. Once there, you may see, a book and be able to read the writings of your past present and future, as well as all of your past lives. Or you may get to hear a master talking to you about all of it. You could even see it as it plays out, sort of like watching a movie. There have been many variations of how the Akashic Records are revealed. Caution here, it is forbidden to snoop just for being nosy. Pure intent is a must.

Automatic writing is another way to access information. Sit quietly; call upon Spirit, surround yourself with the White Light of Christ and your chosen protection. With pen & paper in hand ask a question. Jot down any thoughts that come to mind. Don't think about them; write as if you were taking notes from your supervisor or teacher. Just write.

This is where learning shorthand comes in handy. Some can't open their eyes when channeling so much information. If you knew shorthand, you can jot notes down quickly, as fast as it's coming in. When you're done, and you're reading the information you wrote; you may be amazed at the words and phrases that were used. When it is so different from your own style, you know for sure it is coming from your guide.

The best way to get your own answers is without any outside influences. Keep the intent pure, be in Prayer and have patience. Never ever communicate with guides while under the influence of alcohol or drugs. Yes I know this has been written before; it is here again to stress the point!

Intuition

Before we are born we were all Souls up in Heaven discussing what we will do in this lifetime; to make our Soul leap to the next level. We are up there making plans with everyone we know for which part they will play in the grand scheme of things. Our Mom, Dad, Brothers and Sisters, children, friends and pets have come to play a specific role in your life. Everyone comes into our life for a reason. Some come for a month, a day, or a season and some for a lifetime. You choose this life and everything in it; you are born with this blueprint. The intricate details are all there, right down to the person at the checkout counter at the market who hands you the keys you left behind as you're walking out the door.

Life on Planet Earth is a school. This is where your Soul evolves. Lessons sometimes present themselves by issues and problems. For example: My friend Nikki had a boyfriend who mentally abused her, taking advantage of her by living in her home, eating her food and never contributing to finances or affection. They finally broke up. Year after year, man after man the faces changed but the issues and complaints were exactly the same. It wasn't until Nikki decided to demand self respect and "stand up for herself" that the issues finally went away. She now has a beautiful loving boyfriend who adores every bit of her and is a healthy compliment to their relationship. The moral of this story is: If we don't learn the lessons, they will keep presenting themselves as problems until we "get it". Once we understand why they are in our face, make peace with it and learn the lesson, the problem goes away. (The lesson no longer needs to present itself).

Take criticism with Love for it may be an easy lesson. Always work on making yourself better. The easiest way to identify a lesson is when someone irritates you. Ask yourself what they are "mirroring". What is it about yourself that you do similar to that? They may be mirroring back to you things that YOU do. Ask yourself, "What are they trying to teach you"? The key here is to get it right the first time so you don't repeat mistakes. Be open to all possibilities and be aware of your limiting beliefs. Most of your belief system has been constructed from things you have seen or been told. What we have been told may not be truth, only a belief that has been passed on, maybe even from someone who loves us very much, yet just believed that to be true and it was not.

A story I remember my mom telling me about her friend who cut the ends off the ham before she put it in the oven. She did this because her mother did this. When she asked her mother why she did this; her mother replied, because *my* mother did it. When the grandmother came to visit the question was asked. The grandmother answered "I cut the ends of the ham off because it didn't fit in my pan". Keep this story in mind when you think about why you do certain things; then move the walls of your belief system to transcend all boundaries. Don't say "I don't believe", Say "SHOW ME". Always search for Truth in any and all situations.

There are many different forms of intuition: Clairsentience (feeling/touching); Clairaudience (hearing/listening); Clairalience (smelling); Claircognizance (knowing); and Clairgustance (tasting).

Each one of us processes information in different ways. Some of us are visual people, understanding by looking at pictures. Other people are auditory – having to listen to words in order to "get it". When I work with a client; I speak to each one in the way they will understand. For example: when speaking to an auditory person, I will use words such as "hear what I'm saying" and I might even read something to them. To a visual person I might say something like "look at this situation… as I show them visual diagrams". Because we all access information in different ways, this is how Spirit will talk with us. In the way they know we will find it most useful.

When we identify which way we process information and follow that way, learning becomes much easier. If you're a visual person, you may learn more accurately with pictures in the books you read.

Audio tapes are great for auditory people. Kinesthetic people will benefit from physically doing the activity.

Yummy/Yuck

One of the first ways I identified how to get my own answers was what I call my "yummy/ yuck feeling. How do you know you would *love to eat that pie?* And how do you know that you *'wouldn't be caught dead wearing that shirt'?* There is a specific feeling inside of you that gives you what I call that yummy/ yuck feeling. Play with it; hold that dessert and see where that feeling lives inside of you. See if you can identify what makes it go "yummy" and what makes it go "yuck". Try this when you go to the department store. Hold a shirt next to you, (one that you absolutely hate) and try to identify where in your body it says "NO WAY". This intuition will improve the more you work with it. Have fun with this. Soon you'll find it works on its own and will help you to identify when someone is trying to pull the wool over your eyes.

Barefoot North

The first way of learning how to improve my intuition was 'standing barefoot facing North'. This is when you remove your shoes, face the direction North and cup you hands in front of you at the level of your solar plexus. The idea is to put your question in your hands because your Soul lives one inch - IN and one inch - UP from your solar plexus. It lives right inside your body, right there inside your chest. Sometimes called your Gut feeling and otherwise known as intuition; this seat of the soul is where you'll feel that yummy/ yuck feeling we spoke of in the previous paragraph. When you stand barefoot facing north, holding your hands cupped in front of your solar plexus, take a deep breath in, and upon the exhale close your eyes and ask a simple question which needs a yes or no answer... When you exhale & think "should I eat pizza for supper", you body should list <u>forward for a YES</u> answer, or you will lean <u>backwards for a NO</u>. If at any time you do not move at all, you're probably dehydrated. Try again when you're not. (or place your hands on your kidneys and try it again). This will work with any simple questions. It works wonders at the supermarket. Ask which watermelon will be the most delicious. (Never ask for one to be most ripe, for it may be rotten when you get it home.) Wording is very important. Complicated wording will get confusing where Spirit just won't answer. Keep it short, and keep it simple.

Dowsing

Another way to get your own answers is by dowsing. You can use a pendulum, a necklace with something hanging from it, or even the pull chain from your ceiling fan.

Any weight hanging from a single chain will work. It needs to swing freely without anything in the way.

Hold the pendulum in your hands. Connect with it and blow with a bit of your breath on it on to it to "tell it it's you" and "thank it for giving you the best answers for your highest good". Or you may get interference from the last person who used it… Hold the pendulum in your dominant hand with your thumb, index finger and you middle finger touching the chain. These three fingers complete your energy field to the chain; the pendulum is now an extension of your electrical field. Pull the chain up about two inches and let the heavy part of the pendulum swing free. Hold this over your non dominant hand and ask, "Father/ Mother God, please show me YES". And watch the direction of the swing of the pendulum. Picture the face of the clock so you can decide if the pendulum is swinging from 12:00 to 6:00 or 3:00 to 9:00. Sometimes it will be a clockwise or counter clockwise direction. Take note of this, for this direction is your 'YES'. Say "Thank you" to God/ your higher self and to your pendulum for the answer. Again hold the pendulum the same way and then ask, "Father / Mother God, please show me NO". Then watch to see what direction it swings. This is your 'NO'.

After you have identified the way the pendulum swings for your Yes, and No answers, Then you may begin to ask questions. Always begin with Can I, May I, Should I.

Can I; meaning, am I capable to do this? May I: meaning do I have permission from the Universe/ God to ask this? Should I; is it in my highest and best interest to do this? If and only if you get YES For all three of those questions should you proceed to ask the questions. If you get NO for any of them; stop right there. Begin again tomorrow.

When you first begin to ask questions; keep them short and simple at first. Respect and trust is needed for this to work. Always say 'Thank You' when you receive answers. Gratitude is a must and will result in significant reciprocity of truth.

Do *not* rephrase the question several different ways because you did not like or 'believe' your first answer. This is the sure way to "doubt" and the pendulum will not work for you. It's as if you're saying you don't believe the answer you got. You might as well slap God in the face... Don't bother asking if you don't trust your answer. Go do something else.

Dowsing goes back thousands of years; encyclopedias have it listed as the 15th century in Germany when it was used to find Metals under ground. Commonly known for using Y shaped branches of a tree or L shaped metal rods to find water. According to *www.Wikipedia. org* in the Vietnam war the United States Marines used dowsing in an attempt to locate weapons and tunnels. Today there are many different variations of rods as well as items to dowse for. Many think that dowsing is limited to finding things. Not so. Dowsing is another form of finding answers to any questions you have. It is another way of accessing God or as some would call it "your higher self". You must frame the questions accurately in order to obtain answers and information for anything.

RECIPROCITY

Never take without giving. This completes the circle of reciprocity. Even when you take a rock from mother earth, something should be given in return. Some of my Native friends give tobacco. Some people leave a strand of hair, or fingernail clipping if they don't have tobacco with them. Any type of natural offering is appropriate; as long as it is biodegradable to blend with Mother Earth.

In the field of energy healing, there are many who are in need of a healing who cannot afford to pay your fees. It will be your decision to give a session for free. However, to complete the circle of reciprocity, you must be able to accept a hug as payment, and feel good about it. If you ever sighed when the client left the room, as a motion for (oh joy, now that is not going to pay the bills) then, you're accumulating some karma here. Realize that your thoughts, words and actions must all be congruent for healthy reciprocity. Whatever you accept, you must feel good about it to be complete.

I once had a woman get angry with me that I was charging for my shamanic work. She said, "Shamans shouldn't charge for their gift of healing". I explained that many years ago they didn't charge money because they didn't have to pay for this knowledge. It was gifted to them by their family who were healers before them. Years ago, Shamans were taken care of by the community. They housed the Shaman, fed and clothed him. In Peru, a chicken or Llama was often used as payment for a healing. In the USA we pay for our "studies" with money. Money has become the accepted form of reciprocity in the USA.

Follow your heart and guidance with Love. One does not need to give free healings to prove they work. (Proving you can heal will surely get you into trouble; when Ego rules, you're sure to get mud in your face and literally find yourself in trouble). Reciprocity should be healthy, unconditional gift of giving and receiving with love.

Tarot Cards

Tarot is another tool for obtaining information. Here is just a tidbit of information about Tarot cards just to give you a taste so you can have fun. I suggest finding an expert with integrity if you wish to use Tarot in your practice.

Tarot is a way of divining; it is intense and you must learn how to interpret the answers properly to obtain accurate results. Remember that you are not providing answers to a person's entire life, you are only guiding (with your guidance) to help the person find their own resolution.

There are so many different varieties out there, there are even Angel cards. Begin by saying a prayer while you're shuffling the deck. Have the person you're working with shuffle the cards with one question or dilemma in mind. Then pick a design that appeals to you such as a cross, a pyramid, or circle. Then place the cards on the table in that format. Each card has certain personality traits, and depending upon the order the card is drawn will also help you read if it is in the past, present or future. Also with your issues or desires a time frame for when it may happen may also present itself. Study and get to know the different energies of each card. Once you are familiar with each card, it will present its personality to you. When working with a client you may explain the basic interpretations of the cards; then ask how he or she would apply the meanings to their current situation. As each card is read, the story will begin to unfold. Keep in mind that tarot is like dreams in the relation of interpretation. If you see a red truck in a dream a red truck to you may mean something entirely different than the red truck in my dream. Tarot is similar in the fact that one card presenting an opportunity for new job, may in fact present an opportunity for a new "endeavor" to another client. Some people may want you to tell them what to do; don't be forced into a solid prediction. The cards will give you "opportunities"; after the subject is discussed it is the free will of the person to follow their own path or change it.

You could be tempted to give advice or promise good news for someone who is ill. You never want to influence the outcome of another person, so be responsible. There are many other ways to be encouraging and helpful. Keep your ego out of it; be careful, responsible and work with the utmost integrity. Speak truth and reiterate your client's desires to keep focused. Not going off on a tangent will build rapport between you and your client.

I've had a Catholic friend question Tarot and God. She stated she was scared but curious and didn't want to get God Mad. God doesn't get mad. God guides. God Loves. God Teaches. In my work and communication with Jesus and Mother Mary, they have assured me, when I work in Prayer, Love and the White Light of Christ; with focus for the good of all with pure positive thought, that *is* God. Nothing dark, negative or evil can enter or penetrate through.

My advice is to stay away from Ouiji boards. There is a mixture of energy between you and your friend because it takes two people to run the board. There have been many unhealthy energies playing around these boards. My suggestion is to forget it; do not entertain them. If it's too late & you find yourself with chaos in your life… seek a reputable Shaman for help.

NOW

Focus on the "NOW". Dwelling on yesterday or tomorrow will suck your energy. There are people who play tape loops in their head. Have you ever had a conversation with someone and it later repeats in your head, hours or days after the original conversation or argument took place. This is disempowering and helps no one. Why let things like this drain your energy? Balance and center your Chakras. (See the chapter on Chakras) You'll feel much better and be able to let this go. Only you have the power to control this. Concentrate on what you are doing right at this moment in time and perfection will fall right into place. You'll be amazed at what you can create when you give it your full attention with Love and Light.

Many years ago I took a four hour entrance exam for the Engineering Department at the Electric Company, I filled myself with the White Light then I asked my Spirit Guides & God to come to help me. Out of a possible 104 questions on the test to be answered, I got 104 correct. I amazed myself. During the test I could actually hear the answers in my head and without a doubt which one was right. Working in alignment with Creator can have magical results. Never underestimate what God can do for you. This story should remind you that you are never alone; help is always available from the other side. Call upon the Masters for help at any time; then shut up and listen/see/feel or imagine their presence and let go... The more you do this; the rest will fall into place.

There is power by being in the "Now". Many people multi-task, everything pays the price. Mom would say you're doing things "half-assed". When you work in the now, with Love and Light; concentrate on what you are doing with 100% intensity, the results show the labor of perfection. It shows in the intricate details. People notice. Eckhart Tolle wrote a book about the power of "Now". This book is well worth reading.

Color

Colors feed your Aura. Color harnesses the light, the subtlest of all physical energies. Color can energize, balance and align your body, mind, spirit and emotion. Different vibrational rates of colors have been scientifically registered in addition to the effects colors have on our nervous system. Wear a different color to obtain specific outcomes. Use accents of Emerald green for your office to bring in prosperity and abundance.

Here are some examples:

RED increases energy levels, gives confidence and courage, joy and power.

GREEN heals the heart and promotes peaceful thoughts.

EMERALD GREEN attracts love, fertility, money, prosperity, and wealth.

BLUE represents hope and faith, harmony, peace and tranquility, forgiveness, fidelity, honesty, relieves anxiety and confusion.

INDIGO develops psychic perception, higher intuition, and tranquility.

AQUA can be cool and balancing.

VIOLET increases Spiritual truth, devotion and inspiration.

BURGUNDY is great for wealth, success, prosperity and elegance.

ORANGE increases Courage **BRIGHT ORANGE** for health and vitality.

BROWN gives warmth of the earth, animal magic and home; comfort.

YELLOW stimulates the brain, increases wisdom and helps to focus.

GOLD is good for Prosperity and Spiritual Healing.

DEEP PINK helps marriage, mature love, and trust.

RAINBOW colors bring joy, hope, renewal and balance Chakras

Wearing BLACK all the time will drain your energy. Use a brightly colored scarf to offset this. Experiment and have fun; Colors will brighten your day. Close your eyes and pick a scarf out of a bag, see if you can tell what color it is just by feeling it. Each Color has its own specific vibration. You may be surprised that they do feel different; blue being cool and red feeling warm.

Chakras

Chakras (pronounced cha'-kra' cha as in Charlie, kra as in Kryon) are dynamic energies that represent the mind, body, spirit, emotion; the whole person. Learning about the Chakras will help you understand how they play an important role in your life. Chakras are energy centers in our aura that spin from the physical body extending outward in the energy field (Aura) three inches to sometimes a foot. They are a direct pipeline from our organs and our central nervous system. Healthy Chakras spin clockwise and each has a unique frequency and color. I say clockwise because this is for the majority; there are a few who have a normal spin of counter clockwise. When working with a person, you must check to see which direction is healthy for them and this can be accomplished by dowsing or intuition. There are some people who can actually see these Chakras spinning, others can only sense them. It doesn't matter if you don't see or feel them, as long as you have a general idea of their location.

There are different beliefs about the number of Chakras. We will work with nine Chakras; Seven being on the physical body, the eighth is our connection to Source (Spirit) and the ninth being Spirit itself. Each Chakra identified below has a specific location, a color, element and issue. These archetypes are sometimes used to restore harmony and balance to an individual with an issue.

1st Chakra is located at the base of the spine, between the anus and the genitals. This Chakra is often called the "Root" Chakra. The color is RED - the element is EARTH; associated with Survival.

2nd Chakra is located between two and four inches below the belly button. The color is ORANGE and the element is WATER; associated with Sexuality.

3rd Chakra is located at your Solar Plexus. The color is YELLOW and the Element is FIRE; associates with Power.

4th Chakra is located at your Heart. The color is PINK and/or GREEN and the element is AIR; associated with Love.

5th Chakra is located at your throat where that hollow indentation is at the bottom of your neck. The color is Light BLUE there are no elements associated with this and higher Chakras; this Chakra is associated with Voice and psychic expression.

6th Chakra is located at your third eye approx. one inch above your brow line in the center of your forehead. The color is INDIGO BLUE; associated with Truth.

7th Chakra is located at the top of the center of your head; this Chakra is often called your Crown. The color is Violet; associated with Pure Energy and Universal Ethics.

8th Chakra is 4 to 8 inches above the crown Chakra. The color is Gold; associated with Source of Sacred.

9th Chakra is anywhere between 6 inches to infinity above the crown. The color is TRANSLUCENT WHITE LIGHT; associated with Spirit – the Heart of the Universal God – ONE with ALL of Creation.

Chakras are spinning energy centers that act as processors and transformers helping to regulate vitality and information into the body and brain. They also act as recording centers by locking in the memory of experiences. They are the connection to our spiritual essence and pure White Light.

To open a Chakra, hold your hand approximately two inches above the Chakra, and move two or three of your fingers with your thumb in a counter clockwise manner. To close the Chakra do the same as just stated, only turn your fingers clockwise. To remember this you may think of your kitchen sink faucet; righty tighty - lefty loosey.

By balancing Chakras you can release stress, negativity and any suppressed emotions. Balance the Chakras by opening each one at a time while you are sitting or lying down, clean out any debris (by intending to do so) you can also use a feather to scoop out debris (heavy energy) and always send it to the light for healing and transformation never leave negative energy hanging around. Then place a brightly colored scarf over the Chakra for it to drink in the color, Remove the scarf when you feel complete and close the Chakra before going on to the next one. When all colors have been placed into the appropriate Chakra, fill each one with the White Light of Christ and close them.

Another way to clean out the Chakras is to open one at a time and as you clean it out as above, picture muddy red color coming out of your root Chakra (ALWAYS send it up to the light for healing and transmutation EVERY time you remove negative energy) and installing a bright vibrant red color going into the Chakra. Imagine a muddy orange color coming out of your second Chakra and installing a vibrant beautiful color orange. Imagine muddy or cloudy yellow color coming out of your solar plexus and putting in vibrant beautiful bright yellow. For your Heart you can use green, pink or a combination of green and pink. With your intent remove the muddy, cloudy colors coming out of your heart Chakra, and then install bright vibrant colors of pink and/ or green into your heart Chakra. Continue with removing muddy cloudy colors out and vibrant bright clear clean colors going in. Do this with the remainder of your Chakras in your physical body only one at a time, continuing on with light blue for throat, indigo blue for your third eye, purple for your crown; then above the body with Gold for your 8th Chakra, Translucent White Light for your 9th Chakra.

What you're doing here is cleaning the Chakras by sending the muddy colors up to the heavens for transformation as we spoke of previously and taking the bright colors from heaven filling each Chakra.

Each Chakra will drink in the color and heal the issues associated with it. This can help remove the stresses of our everyday lives and cure the darkest of dis-ease.

Only open one Chakra at a time, or you may feel dizzy. Be sure to close them all before you resume activity. Practice feeling where they are located on the body. You may feel the difference in energy over the Chakra as opposed to other parts of the body such as the arms and legs. Practice sensing the energy while asking yourself what you see/hear/feel or imagine. Is it cold/hot? Does it have substance; wood, metal? What are you sensing?

Imagine a breeze blowing across your hand; would that feel cold, warm, solid, liquid? Use your imagination to make this become a reality. Expand your mind to allow in the essence of creation coming into form.

Please make special note: We *never* leave heavy/ negative energies hanging around; we always send them to the Light/ Heavens for Healing & Transmutation to be changed into Love and Light. Some people send heavy energy or negativity back to the sender, this is only leaving the energy wreaking havoc on earth... only to come back at a later date!!!

Please send all Heavy Energy and Negativity up to the Light/ Heaven to be transformed; so it can rain upon the earth – beautiful, positive energy for the good of all.

Even though this book is meant for you to work on yourself; it will be hard to resist practicing with a friend. An important subject to note here is discretion. Whenever you are working with another person, if you ever detect any energy that may be wreaking havoc in their body, *please* be discrete. There may be a time when you actually begin to read energy and you will know it is cancer, a liver problem, or maybe even Heart disease. NEVER, EVER say this out loud. First, because you are not a medical doctor, and do not have credentials to diagnose. And second, because this will only put the person into a full blown panic. Once the person it in that state of panic, it is difficult to get them fully out. Even if you are a medical doctor or nurse, think about the mental state you'll be placing this client in. It is best to ask them "when is the last time you had a complete check up". Let the final test results speak for themselves. Opinions can be devastating. My friend Kris went to the doctor on a Friday. Based upon her symptoms he told her she may have a brain tumor and needed certain tests. She left that office in disarray and needless to say she was a complete mess until two weeks later when final test results showed there was no tumor. Whether you are a professional medical person, or Alternative healer, please, please, please, use discretion. Always think about how it might affect the person you are speaking to. Think it through thoroughly before you verbalize *any* information out loud. This principal concept should be carried out in all that you do, whether you're reading tarot cards, or repeating channeled information.

Crystals

Crystals come from the earth and are part of God's Creation. Crystals are the ancient ones of our land. Each crystal has its own particular vibration measured in frequencies. Frequency is a measurement of energy. Everything on earth is energy. Energy can not be destroyed; it can only be moved or changed. We are also made of energy. When our energy becomes out of balance we experience dis-ease. Crystals give off a natural healing frequency that is activated by our intention. We can use crystals to put us back into balance and harmony while removing stress. We can use them for healing, protection, programming and more. They can take us to higher states of consciousness and help protect us just by being in our Aura.

Ancient ones that lived before us wore crystals on their bodies for eons. The breastplates of the high priests contained specific Gems and Crystals empowering them. They believed each stone possessed its own powers. Crystals worn in earrings balance your left and right sides. Clusters of Crystals help with group energy. Obsidian stones eat heavy energy and continuously put out positive energy. Even though some say they do not have to be cleansed, I would cleanse them just as a way to say "Thank You" for doing such a great job keeping my space clean & free from harm.

Herkimer Diamonds are beautiful beyond words; they have been known to change chaos into order. But, be careful because if you are a real neat freak but reckless with your thoughts, words & actions this can also change order into chaos. Be very persistent with cleaning Herkimer Diamonds.

My own personal favorite is Selenite. Selenite removes obstacles in your way. It can help you to channel information from your guides more accurately. Yes, Channeling is actually talking with your guides. Did you realize parts of the bible were channeled? When the Angel spoke to Moses, he was channeling. I won't allow my guides to take over my physical body 100%, and neither should you. It's not necessary to get information. Set it up this way when you first begin to communicate. Tell God what you are willing to do, and not.

Selenite structure is made from elongated fibers of gypsum. Place the piece of Selenite with the elongated fibers coming towards you for example: if I was channeling for a friend, I would place a long piece of Selenite on the floor between both of us. If I was alone & wanted to talk with God, I'd have the Selenite standing up in front of me. I've read in several books that Selenite is one of the only crystals that does *not* have to be cleansed, this is incorrect. Selenite absolutely holds energy, and *must* be cleansed as often as you use it. Dowse this out for yourself. Just make sure if you do clean it in water that you don't leave it there for any length of time, Selenite may disintegrate in water. My favorite way to cleanse Selenite is with a mist spray of Florida Water or just pass the Selenite over the smoking sage with a prayer to cleanse sending all impurities to a place that can do **no** harm (of course, to the Light).

Amethyst is a beautiful Purple colored crystal that has tremendous healing properties. Just by having one of these near your bed can facilitate healing while you sleep.

Pendants with Crystals in them attract energy to the wearer. Wands focus energy to a specific place. Pyramids focus and amplify. Crystal Balls have been known to be a window into the future and past. In the days of Atlantis and Lemuria, the High Priests buried crystals with information stored in them. These crystals have now been unearthed. They have been identified as having triangles imbedded in them. You will know it when you see them because there is nothing else like it on the planet. If you find a crystal with such triangle striations, it is sure to be a record keeper. Sit and meditate with it the same way you would contact a Spirit Guide and listen to what it has to tell you. Remember to bring a notebook because you may be writing for hours.

When the human body is out of balance, as in a stressful state; a Crystal healing can help to restore balance and harmony. The healer will place specific crystals in your aura while you relax. During this time the body absorbs the frequencies of the crystals and harmony can be restored. The placement of certain Crystals on certain Chakras will also help balance and harmonize the body, mind, spirit and emotion.

"Love is in the Earth" by Melody is one of the most accurate books about Crystals and Gems on this planet. If you are going to work with Crystals in any way, be sure to read this book from cover to cover; I highly recommend that you have this in your library.

Cleaning crystals

A few important points to mention about crystals: Be sure to wash them thoroughly when you get one; because they can hold programs and collect heavy energy from where they traveled to get to you. Honestly, if you have a Crystal in a room where there's been an argument – it can hold that negative vibration for years. Washing them under clear cold water with the intent to remove any heavy energy and cleanse is sufficient enough to clean them. You can also use the smoke of Sage to cleanse them. Similar to the way you would cleanse your home as we spoke about in the previous chapters. Get to know everything about your crystals; some are sensitive to water, others' sea salt. Some are too soft and may deteriorate. Be observant in how they react with the elements and treat them with respect. All Crystals have a personality and you can develop a rewarding relationship with them.

You can charge or program any crystal with Love and Light by praying with it and telling it what job you need it to accomplish. You can awaken your crystal by playing music, or using Tibetan bells or chanting. Of course, if I said it once I'll say it a thousand times "you must be in Prayer and filled with the White Light of Christ' to make sure the Light and ONLY the Light goes into the crystal.

If you do this with anger or an attitude, look out; I don't want to think of the repercussions.

Specific placement of certain crystals in your home, office, room or desk will direct certain energies to those locations. Be sure to look for the crystal with the proper attribute you wish to attain in which corner of the house.

Did you know that when a Quartz Crystal is squeezed, it emits power? Literally, this can be measured. Pizoelectric is the name for this. These tiny squeezed quartz crystals are what make your watch tic. No wonder they hold so much energy!

All Crystal can be programmed. If you would like to remember your dreams: You will need a real Crystal wine glass. Fill it with pure clean water (NO CITY WATER because it has fluoride) get into your prayer mode and hold the glass of water as you tell it to remind you of your dreams upon waking; then drink half of the water. When you wake in the morning, drink the rest of water. Make sure you have pen & paper handy because the information of the dreams you had will come in so quickly you'll want to remember it all. You may even recall several dreams.

You can program a crystal for almost anything. My niece was having difficulty focusing in school. She would panic when it came to taking tests. In prayer, I programmed the crystal in this way: First by cleaning it to remove any previous programs and heavy energy it may have picked up along the way (as previously discussed). During this procedure I dowsed out all answers using my pendulum. When Dowsing; always ask,

Can I, May I, Should I - to make sure it is in your highest and best interest. And do not proceed unless all these three are answered yes.

I asked the crystal if it would like to help Jen and if it was in her highest and best interest for me to program this crystal. When I got a yes, I knew that crystal was the right one for the job. If I had gotten a "no", I would have kept looking for the proper crystal. I then prayed with the crystal "Father/Mother God, Creator of all there is, I now program this crystal for Jennifer to give her the wisdom needed to pass all tests she wants and needs to take; Thank you, and so it is, and so be it, and it is done. You must believe it with every morsel of your being that the program is correct and that the crystal will now do the job you have assigned it. IF NOT, forget it. It won't work. When I gave my niece the Crystal, I told her to have it with her when ever she was taking a test. She aced school with flying colors and became a nurse.

I've had non believers challenge me. My answer to their questions is: Does it matter if the crystal holds the program or not? What matters is that the required result worked! Is it mind over matter, or is it actually the programmed crystal? Remember there were people who once believed the earth was flat, it didn't change the fact that the earth was round. Never say "I don't believe"… Say "Show me". Open yourself to new possibilities.

NEVER EVER let your beliefs LIMIT YOU or your Healing.

Egg Healing

At this time I would like to share with you a very powerful healing that you can do for yourself. It is called Egg Healing. You will need a private space without interruption until you have completed the session and several Organic Fertilized Eggs. Dowse out the number of eggs you will need before you proceed. Depending on the severity of the illness, injury or situation, you may need a very large number of eggs. Please note, they must be fertilized; unfertilized eggs will not work.

Connect with God and get into your deepest prayer. Ask God to protect you and guide you through this entire process. Remove your clothing and very gently take one egg. Start with your head and move the egg over every square inch of your body, your hair and skin and eventually you will have done this all the way to your fingers, fingernails & toes. So, beginning with your head, hold the egg in your hand and rub the (outside of the egg) shell over your skin; when you get to a place where it does not move smoothly over the skin, stop (I call this the place where the egg sticks). See/ feel or imagine the egg sucking out any dis-ease, impurities or heavy/ negative energy as you roll the egg counter-clockwise in that area as you thank it for removing all these impurities. Then put the egg (gently) in a basket being very cautious not to break it. (You don't want these heavy/ negative energies in your home!) Take the second egg and begin exactly where you stopped with the first egg and continue along the body until it gets stuck again; repeat the same procedure as you did with the first egg, stopping where it got stuck and moving it counter clockwise, etc... Continue this whole procedure in prayer and communication with the egg and God for guidance along the entire body, including that space between the fingers and toes. For Cancer or any serious illness it is not uncommon to use up to 100 eggs, so it is best to dowse out how many you will need before you begin. When the whole body has been scanned with eggs, say a prayer of thanks and get dressed. Then bring the basked of (used) eggs and bury them deep into Mother Earth (caution not to break them; if you break or crack an egg during this process a Clearing Ceremony must be performed). By now you probably already figured out I do everything in Prayer. This assures my protection in every way and I wish to extend this protection to you. So, again in Prayer, dig a hole, bury the eggs and cover. Cover with at least 6 inches of dirt over them to assure animals do not dig them up. Give Thanks to God, Mother Earth for mulching the Heavy/ Negative energy and transforming it into fertile soil.

CLEARING CEREMONY FOR CRACKED/ BROKEN EGGS

In the exact location where egg was broken or cracked, open sacred space. Connect with God in Prayer and call in the <u>Spirit Doctors of Love and Light:</u> from the South, when facing South, turn to the West and call in the <u>Spirit Doctors of Love and Light</u> from the West, turn to the North while calling in <u>Spirit Doctors of Love and Light</u> from the North, turn to the East calling in the <u>Spirit Doctors of Love and Light</u> of the East, then look up to the Heavens and call in the <u>Spirit Doctors of Love and Light</u> from Heaven, and then look to the Earth, and call in the <u>Spirit Doctors of Love and Light</u> of Mother Earth. This puts you in a circle of Love and Light guided by God. As you stay within this circle; Ask God to remove any heavy/ negative energies present and bring them to the proper dimension where they can be healed and transmuted into Love and Light. Give Thanks to God, and the <u>Spirit Doctors of Love and Light</u> from each direction upon closing this ceremony.

Special note: After any illness or injury is cleared; you must maintain a balance of Mind/Body/Spirit/Emotion & Soul... What this means is that, when you have removed an illness such as cancer, you must then follow a path of eating pure organic, Non-GMO (genetically modified) foods. You cannot return to a life of eating junk food, or food that has been injected with antibiotics, sprayed with pesticides or altered in any way. Your food intake must be pure.

If you have removed heavy/ negative energy, you cannot engage in gossip to trash your neighbor; the heavy negative energy will come back to you quicker than a magnet attracts iron.

It wouldn't be right to speak about the Laws of the Universe without giving recognition to Dr. Norma Milanovich and Dr. Shirley McCune who wrote "The Light Shall Set You Free". This is by far one of the best books I have ever read. It explains in passionate detail; our Universal Laws and how to abide by them. The first time I read this book, I couldn't put it down. I read it in one weekend. Then I read it again, chapter by chapter. And when that was done, I picked up the book a third time and read a paragraph at a time so I could digest it even further. Now I keep it by my favorite chair to read sections over again. It is genuinely food for your Soul. This book contains the greatest spiritual teachings from the ancient mystery schools with instructions on how to apply those teachings in your everyday lives in addition to the many wise words of wisdom from the Ascended Masters. The first time I read the italicized words that were channeled from the Ascended Masters – My crown Chakra was spinning so fast I thought I was going to levitate. Here is a quote from The Light Shall Set You Free: "Once the decision is made to begin receiving the Language of Light, the initiate must purify the body, mind and Spirit. This is accomplished through discipline and will. It is at this time that the disciple is shown the way to clear all karmic debts and he or she begins to accrue desirable Karma for the future."

We must remember that the plan is much bigger than we are. We get so caught up in our everyday worlds with who said what, about who and why she did that! It's like quicksand. We forget about being one with all. We forget about the blueprint we were born with. We need these Laws of the Universe to remember why we're here. It would be in your best interest to get this book by Dr. Milanovich & Dr. McCune. Your Spiritual path will enhance significantly.

Kryon

Lee Carroll channels Kryon and has written many books in this regard. The series of eleven of these books are very inspiring to help you understand what life is all about. As written on Kryon's website www.kryon.org

I am honored to quote Lee Carroll: *"We believe that God did not stop speaking to humans 2,000 years ago. To think that God stopped communicating is to deny your own divinity, or to assign some special sacredness to the past, not feeling worthy to consider yourself part of God's continued plan for an enlightened Earth. You are worthy of a continued communication with God... which I teach is actually a part of YOU!*

But there is something that comes with channelling...

Responsibility!

Anyone can channel, and Spirit is not proprietary in this regard. It's for all Humans, and not just a few. Therefore the ability and potential exists for this attribute for us all. Like so many other things, INTENT of the human means everything. Not all channelling is given with PURE INTENT. Therefore, some is real, and some is not... and YOU should be able to tell the difference when you HEAR or READ it. Is it really from Spirit? **Channelling Definition: The divine, inspired words (or energy) of God as imparted to Humans by Humans."**

Something to think about:

I used to live in that 3rd dimensional reality of *living life in the fast lane*, driving a Corvette, wearing the newest styles & latest Fur coat with Diamond jewelry accessories. Working every day with blinders on, getting caught up in the gossip of the many. I was the True 'Material Girl'. It took a fall that broke my back and many doctors who couldn't help for me to seek alternative ways of healing… This began my spiritual journey into the 4th dimension. (For years I spent many days traveling back & forth between 3rd & 4th dimensions with Ego as my vehicle.) Then gradually I began to shed the Ego self & spend more time in my God Self (the 4th Dimension). As a Lightworker, I am responsible for 12,000 to plant a seed in each one of them, to awaken them to the Light, for when the time is right. (The timing for them to jump to the 5th dimension).

Working with our God self, Ascended Masters, Angels Saints & Helper Guides is how we will gain entrance to Ascension. It is with their help that we can transform our selves from our ego based consciousness to one of complete bliss with Divine Intervention & God's Guidance.

I believe the year 2012 will bring Ascension for those who are ready. This is the "EARTH Changing as we know it" – yes the Earth will change, but mostly it is the consciousness that will change and we can catch a glimpse of this every day when we witness people talking about spirituality. Ascension will be to the 5th dimension; the place where Ego is completely non-existent and all will be connected to their God self. They will walk in alignment with the Universe each & every day. Everyone will know that we are truly one with God and that we are Co-Creators of Life, living with Unconditional Love for all. (All being humans, animals, plants, rocks, mother earth, the Universe).

Most people go through living their lives day after day. When things are hunky dorey & they don't connect with spirit the way they should. They follow the easy, fun path and only call on Spirit when in NEED! This is what I call a hole in our Auric systems as humans. This is hole and many have not repaired it because they have neglected it for so long they just can't see it!

Truly, most people don't pray until they are in NEED of something changing in their lives, and that, most sadly is at a time when something has hit them in the gut; like divorce, death, or an illness that is really devastating. Then they turn to Creator/ God & beg for help. When in reality they have neglected Creator.

Healing

All this talk about Healing; there are as many healing techniques as there are ideas in the world. People from all walks of life have channeled, experienced or invented different types of healings. The key is to find one that you can incorporate into your life with grace and ease. If you have to work very hard at something, or it does not come natural, then you probably won't stick with it. Find something you enjoy and it will become a blessed part of your life; enhancing and raising your Soul to higher levels each and every day. Once you decide to follow a Spiritual path, Spirit will guide you forward. Question any teacher who moves backwards or does not enhance their spiritual growth.

Dr. Usui

If you want to be a healer, my suggestion is to begin with Reiki. Reiki has come to us from Sensei Mikao Usui from Japan. He taught the 'hands on healing' a form of channeling the Universal (God-force) energy to activate the body's ability to heal itself. The process of learning Reiki begins with something called an "Attunement". To put it simply, this is a way of the Reiki teacher, teaching the student how to energetically recognize the vibrations of Reiki. Once the vibrations are recognized (within the aura) by the Student, the Reiki Teacher explains the positions of the hands. 'Self-healing' and how to perform healing with people, pets, plants, situations and more.

Class Outline

A good Reiki teacher will have a class outline similar to this...

First in prayer, before students arrive the teacher will create a sacred space for people to work. This aligns the energy of the space and assures that negative energies stay away from the class. An introduction should include identifying fire exits, bathrooms and where drinks can be found. Each student should have an opportunity to introduce his or herself. Handouts should include information such as: a clear picture of symbols, an outline of what to expect during the course, what time breaks will be and what time class is over. The history of Reiki should be described as well as the Lineage from Sensei Mikao Usui to the teacher of the class. The teacher should also explain where your name will appear on the list when *you* become a Master (to distribute to your own students one day). Reiki 1, Reiki 2 and Master should be defined so the student knows exactly what the entire program entails. The teacher should talk about all Legal Aspects. Especially that Reiki people cannot diagnose, prescribe or indicate there are any health issues with the client. As NON-Licensed health care practitioners, you must leave that area to the Medical Professional. Know the Laws in your City/State and abide by them. When the Symbols of Reiki are taught, the student should be allowed to practice until they are comfortable with them. Symbols are used to enhance the energy of Reiki. Energy, Aura's and Chakras' should be explained in detail; how to open Chakras, clean and close them. Reiki is Universal (God-force) Energy. Each student should be trained how to see/feel/read energy during this class. It is important to learn how to identify negative energies and how and where to find someone who can remove them when you're in over your head. Students education should include give and receive sessions under the guidance of the teacher until they are comfortable with doing it alone. Everyone should be reminded about basic hygiene. Nothing should be taken for granted, for example: The student should be reminded **not** to chew gum, not to smell like cigarettes, to have clean breath and *never* breathe in the client's face. Keep your finger nails clean and short (and toe nails if you wear open toed shoes). Always tie your hair back and make sure you and your clothes are washed and smell clean and tidy. When giving a session; placing hands on the throat area is a delicate area. Make sure not to press hard on the throat. Most importantly; I can't stress this enough… **keep one eye open at all times** so you can watch the clients face, body language and breathing. A lot of Reiki practitioners try to read the body with their eyes closed. One student of mine was moving her hands during a practice session and almost put her hand on a man's private! Had I not moved her, it would have been very embarrassing. A client's facial expressions, clenched fist and breathing will tell you if they are uncomfortable with anything you are doing. Before each session, assure the client that it is okay to stop at any time. When the session is over, gently touch their arm and tell them so. Ask them how they are feeling. Stay within arm's reach until they sit up & are off the table. Remind them to drink lots of water. Any time someone works in your energy field it is best to drink water. This grounds them and will help flush out any toxins that may have come up during the session. Let them talk about their experience if they want to, if not, thank them for allowing you to be a part of this session. If they wish to make another appointment, do so before they leave. Welcome any feedback they may have. Constructive criticism is a great way to fine tune your skills; take them with gratitude. Testimonials say more than any advertisement when it is written from the heart.

Mystery

Some Reiki practitioners like to keep Reiki mysterious, as if they are performing some sort of magic healing. Reiki is Universal. Anyone can do it. Although it should be treated as sacred, you do not have to be special to learn Reiki. Ego will surely kill the Reiki energies, so it is best to stay humble if you want them to soar. Never let anyone think it is secretive or special; these thoughts keep Reiki in the "voodoo, and weird categories" and that helps no one. When anyone asks about Reiki, educate them with facts. Never elaborate with miracle cures, this will gain attention and trouble. Trouble because not every healing will be miraculous. Healing is not always "living"... it may also include crossing over with grace and ease when the client is ready. More on this later...

RULES

Each student will developed their own techniques that work for them. A good set of rules are the standard code of ethics that can be printed from the IARP (International Association of Reiki Practitioners) website. It is not necessary to use crystals, candles, music or bells. Tools such as these offer energy, they do not do the healing. God does the healing. Nothing offers more energy than God. Do I use tools? Yes, because they are fun and I like them. Do I need them? Absolutely not; all I need is a solid connection to God to do the work. If you're driving down the road and an accident has just happened, you can literally Reiki the man on the ground (with his permission of course) until the Rescue comes. Reiki can be plain and simple or as ceremonial as you like. When you approach each client with pure positive thought, unconditional Love in your heart and God on your side, healing will take place. When giving a Reiki session, you become a conduit (pure open clear pipeline) for God's healing energies to come from Heaven to the Client. As you ground these energies to the Earth the (client) body's innate ability to heal takes over and healing is accelerated. Remember it is not you doing the work. It is all God's work taught to us by Sensei Usui, all in Divine Order. Although Jesus was the first hands on healer, many have come after him. Sensei Usui has awakened this dormant art of healing and brought it into our lifetime.

Integrity

Not all teachers are proficient in their work. Not all teachers walk their talk, or work in integrity. This is where you will need to be diligent in finding the proper teacher who can help guide you to a higher level. When you search for possible teachers, dowse it out. Go with your intuition when asking in your mind, 'who is the best teacher for me to study Reiki with?' Call the teacher. Interview them on the phone. Ask for credentials. Who did they study with? For Reiki, Sensei Usui lineage is a must. 'Lineage' is the list of people who Sensei Usui taught, from the very first person he attuned who was Chujiro Hayashi then Hayashi attuned Mrs. Hawayo Takata, (who brought Reiki to America) and she attuned her granddaughter Phyllis Lee Furumoto and so forth… the lineage list would have all those names in order from who attuned who all the way starting with Dr. Usui, to your teacher's name being on the bottom of the list. The best teacher would be one who was closest to Sensei Usui. Not the twenty-fourth removed.

Remember that telephone game? The one where someone whispers in your ear, then they tell the person next to them, and so forth until the tenth person at the end of the line speaks the statement aloud for all to hear? Most times the statement said aloud is not even close to the one whispered in the first person's ear. This is what happens with information; the most accurate comes closest from the Source.

Experience

It has been documented that we as humans only retain a portion of what is taught in class. People usually add their own life experiences to fill in the rest. The end result is not always good. When studying 'Healing', Reiki or any form of Energy work; it is best to have your own inner guidance and connection with God to guide you. Search for a teacher with integrity who *continues* to study and raise their own levels of Spiritual growth. They don't have to be attending school; study can come in from Heavenly realms as well. Stay away from the arrogant know it all's; you don't need to feed their ego. Interview your prospective teacher to see how long it took them to get from Reiki 1 to Master? How many years of experience did they have between levels Reiki 1 and Reiki 2, and Master?

Because we have a connection to the World Wide Web; it is easy for us to search a person's name. When searching, notice what comes up as you type their name… after typing their name in the search engine, add words such as "complaint", "spam", "corruption", "trickery", "fraudulence", "deceit". Any website that has complaints against this person will surely come up. Remember to also search for good; adding the word "recommendations" after the teachers name should reveal good results. Read everything you can before choosing your teacher. You won't be sorry when you do this in Prayer.

The best teachers will teach you how to get your own answers and how to heal yourself, others want to be the guru & have you go to them for everything. Watch for signs of this in everyone you interview. See how much they encourage and guide you to fulfill your dream. The ultimate teacher is one who rejoices when the student has surpassed the teacher.

When you've chosen your teacher; approach the subject with an open mind. Each lesson comes to us for our higher good to raise us up to new levels in our Soul's growth. And remember, just because you learned it this way today, does not mean those teachings are absolute. Energy changes and teachings change based on the student's readiness to improve, the times of Earth, and Spiritual Guidance. A good teacher knows who is guiding her at all times. Don't be afraid to question this. A teacher who continues to say "Creator said *this or that*", without a moment of hesitation to double check where the guidance is coming from, should be avoided. Acknowledgement for the messages to and from Spirit, are important even from the most adept Teacher. Many people claim to Channel. Many people talk non-stop with the words "creator said". You will have to use discernment in all things that you do and say.

Modalities

Years later when you have Mastered Reiki and are ready to move on to another form of healing search for the appropriate modality to appeal to you. It may be Massage, Reflexology, Cranial Sacral therapy, or Shamanism. There are many modalities out there. When you approach each one with Love in your heart, pure positive thought with a prayer, you Guidance will help you all the way. God will surely find something you love and guide you through it to be of service to humanity. (Of course if this is your divine path). The more you give thanks, the more good things will come.

Community service is a great way of showing gratitude. Humbly giving 10% of your income to charity is also a Heavenly way of giving back for the healthy circle of reciprocity. If you want this to work; don't brag about it, just do it!

In order to be a good healer you must always work in integrity. This means being so squeaky clean that you'd welcome the presence of The Blessed Virgin Mother Mary and not be ashamed for anything you *think*, *do* or *say*. It means do the healing and get out of the way. Know that it is God doing all of the work through you. You are acting as a conduit (that means empty pipeline without judgment) with the healing energy coming through you. If you have an opinion while doing the healing work… it will sabotage it. If you perform an excellent healing and the next day get on the phone to brag about it… it will sabotage it. All of your hard work will be erased. If you go home and search for proof; for example, calling the client to see how they are, basically looking to see/hear or find confirmation that the healing took place… it will sabotage it.

Prepare the Space

The atmosphere must be clean in order for healing to take place. Prepare the space, energetically by clearing yourself, then those closest to you, then the home or building and grounds around it. Include the entire property before the client steps foot into your space. If you were to draw a diagram of what this would look like, you'd have concentric circles. In the center would be you, then next would be the person you live with (such as a spouse) closest to you, and then next person close to you (each of your children), then one of these circles would be the home or building where you would be doing your healing work, then lastly would be the property or grounds that the building lives on. Every day, clearing begins with you, then in order of closeness, those who live with you, and finally the home and grounds. This is like building a house. The foundation is most important. If there is a flaw in the foundation the whole house will come down. It is the same analogy. If you have an issue/ entity, or something that is OFF center; there is no sense working on another person. The healing won't work. You must be completely clear in order to progress to the levels of healing another person. If not, you can actually do more damage than good.

Healings gone wrong

I've had many clients come to me with what I call *horrific healings gone wrong.* One specific woman (We'll call her Ann) called me to ask if I could help, she was in terror and crying. She had gone for a Reiki session in another town about half an hour from my place. The Reiki practitioner told her she had an entity, her home was possessed and her family had demons. This poor woman was frantic. Ann went on to say the practitioner's eyes got big, (as if scared) and she told her to leave her office. I let her tell me her story and immediately I assured her we could take care of this "right now". I put her on hold for a minute while I energetically removed her fear then talked with her in a calm voice until she relaxed. When she hung up; I went to work on this situation. First clearing her, then her husband, each of her children, her home, the grounds she lived on and then went on to clear the *entity* of the Reiki practitioner who created this panic.

Many years ago I was asked to help out a woman who held a Reiki clinic at the local church. She said too many people signed up and she only had three practitioners to give sessions. I had already become a master and was seeing my own clients; at this point I was very experienced. I enjoyed a feeling of giving back to the community; this was instilled in me by all of my teachers with integrity. (It enhanced the circle of reciprocity). There were four massage tables behind a huge curtain so there was some privacy. A tiny radio played soothing music off in the distance. None of the massage tables had sheets or blankets on them. None of them had pillows. And none of them had a step stool for short people to climb onto the table. What I saw this day showed me how many people really don't know what they are doing. Let me explain more. An elderly lady jumped onto the massage table and almost fell off to the other side. The practitioner was on the other side of the room. There was no pillow for her head no pillow or roll for under her knees, no sheet on the table and nothing to cover her with. During the session I watched the practitioner proceed to do Reiki on her *without* touching the client. Yes, it is true, you don't have to touch each client in order for Reiki to work, but I wonder if this practitioner ever had a Reiki session given to her? The only time I would not touch would be a burn victim. People like to be touched. It makes them feel safe. It is much easier and comfortable for both the client & practitioner to have the light touch of hands than to hold them six inches above the body. Anyone watching this would think the client had bugs and the practitioner was afraid she'd catch them. At the end of the session, the practitioner walked to the radio to change the station while the elderly lady fell off the massage table! I was too far away to stop this. All I could think was 'where on earth did this woman learn how to do Reiki'? The shame of it all is that there are so many practitioners out there just like this. They don't have a clue what they are doing!

During a class on Soul Retrieval students were practicing on each other. As Mary worked with Sam, you could clearly see Mary trying to coax Sam to do the work. The more Mary tried to assure Sam he was in good hands, the more uneasy he got. I print this issue here as a reminder to watch the body language of the client at all times. Clearly Sam was not ready to heal that issue. Had Mary been observant of his clenched fists and sweaty brow, she would have stopped this before it got ugly. If this was Mary on the table, she would have approached the subject and 'ripped it off quick like a band-aid". But this was not Mary. It was Sam and he was clearly not ready to go there.

One woman told me she was giving a Reiki session and the client fell asleep, she said she had to pick up her son at school, so she left the client sleeping on the massage table. NEVER! I repeat NEVER, ever leave a client unattended! This is not professional at all.

Make sure you have ample time for a session, or don't do it! As a healer, I would never leave a client in a worse place than they came in. Sometimes this takes an hour, sometimes four. Everyone is different. If you don't have that time to work with a client; do something else. Maybe healing is not for you.

It took me five years to obtain my Reiki Master/ Teacher Certificate. Some people are now taking a crash course where they can learn Reiki 1, 2 and go home with Master Certificate all in one weekend. And they are told they can teach as a Master. The problem is they are given the material and left on their own to figure the rest out. Not everyone has supreme guidance and obviously some are missing common sense in the department of integrity and ethics.

Surely you will come into some heavy energy if you are going to do healing work. You will know when someone has Cancer. There is no energy that feels like it in this world. You will know when you've come in contact with something from the dark side. Whenever you sense something bad with a client; **NEVER, EVER tell them** they have a demon, entity or some evil spirit! REMOVE IT FIRST... Then if you must feed your ego, tell them *when it is gone*! Telling a client they have something evil will surely put them into a tailspin. Most people will not be able to even think rationally after being told they have a demon. What can you accomplish after that? NOTHING! Have compassion here, call upon God, clear the heavy energy, and get to work on the important issues. You should always have two people to turn to when you get in over your head. Make sure these two can remove the darkest of the dark when you need help. Hold yourself straight in your center, fill yourself with the White Light of Christ and get to work as we discussed in the pages of this book. You will not get a pat on the back for removing evil; if you choose to do this type of dance I suggest you prepare yourself thoroughly. The first book I would encourage you to read is by my friend David Ashworth. The name of his book is "Dancing with the Devil as you channel in the Light". This book is for everyone working with people, *especially healers*, working hands on or not. And if you have the opportunity to be in the UK, look him up and take a class with him. The next person I suggest you work with is Raymon Grace. He has a unique way of shifting energy from negative, to Positive Love & Light. Raymon Grace's book is "Techniques that work for me". Both David and Raymon's techniques are affective and accurate. I highly recommend both of these men because they work in the highest integrity of Love and Light.

There are a few rules for every practitioner who works with a client on a massage table, and wants to do healing work of any kind. Read the next section three times and know it back and forth.

Session details

It begins with a phone call. The client will call you to set up a session. (On the phone, be courteous. Give the client time to talk. Never be in a hurry. Give the client a choice for a couple of sessions. Take their name and contact phone number. No one expects emergencies, but they do happen. And write it in your calendar. (The one you look at daily!)

Never book a session for a friend. Many people call thinking you can fix their friend/spouse/mother or father. Unless the friend/spouse/mother or father is physically incapable of speaking to you on the phone, that is different. It is best to speak with the person you will be working with, and only them. When you have them on the phone, their energy will prepare you for their visit and your intuition will kick in right away. Always take notes for your own accuracy, this reinforces intuition. Even if a friend refers the client to you NEVER discuss the client or what happened in a session.

Before the client comes; make sure you've cleared yourself, those close to you, your working space (the whole building, not just the office) where you will see the client, and the grounds (property of the building); after each one is cleared; fill with White Light of Christ to seal. (So good energy seals in and bad energy stays out!) If you forget one of these clearings and sealing, the foundation will be weak and something negative may get in. Be diligent in your work. It can save your life. Yes, this information has been placed here again. This is the clearing/white light concentric circles we spoke of earlier. USE them to protect yourself and keep your clients safe.

Check the place where the client will park; is it safe? If it is at night, is it clearly lit? Is the path to your office clean and clear? If not, fix it.

You will need to prepare the healing room; household cleanliness is a must, especially for the lavatory. Make sure you have clean water available if they need a drink and box of tissues if they need to cry. Watch your use of perfume, candles, incense or other things can have a scent. Some clients have allergies. Make sure all pets are put away and client is not allergic. Never clutter your healing space. It may be wise to do some research in Feng Shui. Denise Linn wrote a great book called "Sacred Space". This can help prepare and keep your healing space energetically sound. The healing space should also be climate controlled at a normal temperature. This is for the client; not you. So if you're having hot flashes get the proper herbs to get over that and adjust temperature for clients. People often get cooler when lying down; keep them comfortable at all times.

Have the massage-table already set up, legs locked in place that is comfortable for your height. The head of the table should be facing North or East for the best energetic work. Clean cotton sheets, one fitted for the bottom, allergy free pillow with cotton pillow case for under the head, a roll pillow for under the knees (keeps weight off the spine) allows the client to lie on back for longer periods of time without stress. Use a light top cover cotton sheet for summer and add a blanket for winter months on top of client (ask them first). The light sheet and blanket are to make the client feel secure so they do not feel so exposed. A small step stool should be available for clients that need a boost up onto the table. No one should ever be expected to "hop-up". Always be within an arm's reach for someone getting up onto or off of the table. It doesn't take much for someone to get dizzy after lying down if they rush to get up. Be ready to grab their arm to steady them and help at all times.

When the client comes, give them time to settle in, have them shut off all cell phones, use rest room if they need to, fill out a form that you can keep on file with their information and any notes you may wish to keep. This will help you remember them and their healing progress. At this point they should be given a statement saying *what to expect from a session with you* in the next few days with your contact number in case they have any questions. While they are reading this is the time for you to wash your hands. Make sure your phone is off so there will be no interruptions. All of these details show the client you are meticulous. The last thing you want during a session is a distraction of any kind. Interruption disturbs the energy and throws everything off. It can take an hour or more to recover after the energy has been upset.

Occasionally I will have a client show up for a session with a family member or friend. I will allow them both to enter the healing space for conversation but rarely will I allow another person to watch; this not a show. This work is Sacred and is between the Client, his/her Spirit Guides, Angels, Saints, and God. One never knows what will take place during a healing session. In order to allow the maximum opportunity for God to work on what is needed, we need to hold energy as Sacred space. When a friend comes to watch, their energy is different and interferences can complicate issues. It is best to have this discussion when the client calls. That way there are no surprises.

While the client is seated on a couch or chair, sit across from them. Energetically show them know you are not in a hurry; relax. Energy can be read by many people; never think you are the only one reading it. A client will know if you are nervous, fearful or tired.

Let the client tell his or her story. Each client will have their own way of explaining what happened to them. Everyone has a story. For this area of the session it would be beneficial to be skilled in Hypnotherapy and NLP (Neuro-Linguistic). This would help you read and understand the signs of the body. Many times the client is telling you one thing and his/ her body is saying something quite different. Energy and Body language is a big help in sorting out exactly what is wrong and where to begin.

For example, many times a person will come in with Carpel Tunnel and explain how they type on the computer for hours on end... when in reality it is because they are lacking in self-love. Many times the physical injury is not the problem. It could very well be on another layer of Mind/Spirit/Emotion or Soul. It could even be a past life thing. Be a good listener when the client is talking. You may want to use some of their words (just a few) to let them know you are listening. Here you will want to note whether they are talking in auditory words/ visual words, or are they kinesthetic in how they access information. This information will help you later when you need to explaining things to them. Do not insult their intelligence by repeating one word from each sentence... this is not what I'm talking about here. NLP will teach you details in this subject.

Ask the client *if* they would like to get on the massage table. Do not assume. Some people prefer you work on them while they sit in a chair as opposed to them lying down. For a scheduled appointment you would not work on the floor. This is awkward for them as well as you. No one wants someone climbing over them during a professional setting. When they choose to get on the massage table, have them remove their shoes and have them use the step stool to help them up. Be sure to tuck the stool under the table while you are working around the table so you don't trip over it during the session.

It is best to connect to God to begin channeling the Reiki energies with their head in your hands. Give thanks to the guides who help you every day such as Jesus, Mother Mary and Ascended Masters; thank them in advance for their guidance and help in this healing session. This assures you have constant open connection with accurate information coming in. Also (in your mind, it doesn't have to be stated aloud) give thanks at this time to Sensei Usui for awakening Reiki and bringing it forth to humanity as you ground the energy coming through you to the Earth. At this point your

Angels, Saints, Spirit Guides & God will begin talking with the Client's Angels, Saints, Spirit Guides & God. This is a good time to tell the Client it is okay for them to go to their happy place and relax, it is also okay for them to sleep if they wish. As they relax; listen quietly for any communication that may be going on from your intuition and Guidance. Keep in mind when you get information, to first be sure you know *where it is coming from.* Then ask your guides if it is in your best interest to say this information to the client. And also include asking to see if it is in the client's best interest at this time for you to say it to them. Is it in the highest and best interest of all involved? And of course, make sure it is within your legal rights. If you are not a doctor, you have no medical rights to diagnose, etc…

During the session, follow your guidance with love in your heart. Remember every session is sacred. This client trusts you enough to have his life in your hands (energetically), this is truth. Treat this client as if he/she was your first newborn child. Watch for signs from the client at all times.

Look at that physical body with an innocent curiosity and you will be shown ways to help. There may very well be a time where you are shown medical issues. It is not for you to blurt out "oh, look here, what is this?" or "oh my, you have a problem here"… This is not in integrity. If you are not a licensed medical professional you are legally in error here. It is in your best interest to use discretion and the most you can say professionally would be later, after the session is over, to say it is good to have a check up with your doctor. You cannot or should not ever tell a client they have a medical issue. And most importantly, I repeat, never, ever talk about a client you had in your office. As a healer you must adhere to a code of ethics and confidentiality. It will help build your reputation as a professional. Adhering to high standards and codes of ethics will make you act as a professional therefore; fulfilling the role of a professional and this is when you will be treated as a professional. If you are slacking in any of these areas, expect to be treated as such and your work won't be taken seriously. Energy precedes thought; people will read your energy, it tells much more than you could ever say or do.

When the session is complete, place your arm on the client's arm and tell them "the session is now complete". Never walk away leaving them to figure out for themselves that the time on the table is complete. Have the client sit a bit before getting off the massage table while you place the step stool in place for them to use. Sometimes they get up too fast and get dizzy, remind them to get up slowly. Stay within arm's length as they are seated on the couch or chair for further discussion. They may have questions. Answer all of their questions until their understanding is clear and they are complete. Assure them if they have further questions, they may call you (while handing them your business card). Escort them to the door and watch them get in their vehicle if the session was done in your home. (This is good advice given to me by an insurance agent). In an office atmosphere it won't be necessary to do this. This is a good time to note: make sure you have the appropriate *insurance* and coverage for your business and Operating Business license posted on the wall. Again; know the laws and abide by them in your City/State and country for operating a business.

When session is over and client has gone. Clear the room energetically. Clear yourself, check and clear the concentric circles again, starting with you, you loved ones, pets included also if they are present in the building space where this healing took place. Also making sure to clear the building and land then fill each with White Light to seal in the good energy. Change the sheets/pillow cases & pillow case for the roll. Each client deserves new linens even though they are fully clothed during sessions. Linens should smell crisp and clean. Now you are wondering why I would clear concentric circles after each client? This is being diligent. When working with such energy, the brighter the light, the darker the dark wants to extinguish that light. One can never be too cautious when working with energy.

DAD

My eighty year old Father in law was one of my frequent Reiki clients. He was a very strict French Catholic. The very first time he came for a session he told me a woman healer fixed his back when he was twenty years old. He believed in the Healings and wanted to make sure I was doing it right. He proceeded to ask me what God I pray to. Being raised Catholic and attending the same church he did for 30 years; I assured him "Dad, I pray to the same God you do because there is only One." This is when he said "then why don't I hear you when you are reiki'ing me?" From then on I repeated the *Our father* and *Hail Mary* aloud, over & over again for the entire session. I must admit it opened my chakras and Spirit came in as soon as I prayed. My hands became electric, pulsed and got very hot. He could feel it moving the pain right out of his body. It was very intense. Dad continued to come for sessions, he said it renewed him. Until he was 90 years old he rode 2 miles a day on the stationary bike in the house. He loved life and his family and kept us all close with his unending love.

There will come a time in every healer's life when a client comes to them ready to die. When my old father in law was ninety one, he was ready to cross over. He wanted to discuss this in detail. It was heartwarming to be able to comfort him at his time of need. The rest of the family was still at a place of denial. Many would scold him when he mentioned the word death or would tell him not to talk foolishly. I embraced him and worked with him to help him prepare the way so when his time came, he was so comfortable with it, there was no remorse. Each time Dad would come for a session, he would jump up on the table and ask me to pray aloud with him. Then he wanted to talk with God. He wanted to know where he was going and how he could make a deal to come back to communicate with me. We would talk about who was coming to get him, was it St. Jude? Was it Archangel Michael? Then he'd tell me he had questions for certain saints. There was no fighting, no resisting, just total embrace in the life he was going to after this one. Eight months later, Dad died with dignity. My wish is that everyone would embrace death; knowing that it is only crossing over to another side. And to know that we can visit these worlds because the veil is very thing, all we have to do is ask. Too many people fear it and get stuck between the worlds when they actually take their final breath. As a Shaman we were taught to live each day of our life as it was our last; leaving nothing undone. With no unfinished business, we can travel to the Light without hesitation and take our seat next to the Masters. On the day of Dad's death, I was able to perform Shamanic death rites as taught to me by the Q'ero Indians of Peru. This is an elegant ceremony to guide the luminous body to the Heavenly realms. One can actually watch the Light come down, embrace the Aura and raise it up to Heaven. Dad has since come to talk with me, thanking me and assuring me that he is really on the other side of that thin veil. Since his passing, several of the family members have been shown his presence in many ways. It is comforting to know things are at peace here and there as well.

TRUST

One night while driving to my friend Ilka's new house, the navigation device stated "there will no longer be step by step navigation after this point as many of the streets are unknown territory". I thought "*What?*!!!" There was nothing around but cow pastures and there must have been a mile between houses. There was no cell service, no street lights and no people. I had never been here before and it was 11:00 at night. All the gas stations were closed and it literally looked like they rolled up the sidewalks after dusk. Up until now I had been at a Dowser's convention and had planned on sleeping at Ilka's because she lived only a few towns away from the convention. At the point where panic started to creep in, I realized I needed to let go & let god. Of course I was always prepared with jacket/blanket/water and snacks when I traveled. Once I surrendered I began praying "God if this is what you want for me, do what you will…" I felt the process of letting go, watched the light literally surround the car and guide me to the top of the hill. At this point my cell phone beeped with service. I called Ilka and she said "come on down". I was literally at the top of her street. Was that ahhhhhhhh feeling of knowing the Let Go & Let God & the power to trust in him that transmuted chaos into order.

MORE LIGHT

When I began to study Spirituality I knew I needed to work with others who had more light than I did. The brighter my light became, I raised the bar for my teachers. Everyone should study with someone who is, I don't want to say better than they are for those are not appropriate words, what I want to say is find teachers with at least 80% light in the beginning, then you will get to the point where all of your teachers should be in the 95-98% light. Dowse this out for accuracy.

Raising the Light requirement for your teachers will continue to raise you in the Light. This is true for those you socialize with. It is in your highest and best interest to surround yourself with friends of integrity who continue to strive for a greater good. Friends who continue to read/educate/and improve, will inspire you. Friends who are comfortable with their lives, or live in a rut won't grow spiritually. You need inspiration at this point and you deserve the best. Walk your talk and talk your walk. As you raise your vibrations of Love and Light, ask God to attract to you, those who will help to maintain your Light or make it brighter. It is much easier to live and work with like minded souls all working for a higher good, than to fight the chaos and negativity of those struggling to pay their mortgage.

JOY

While working at the Electric Company as a welder, we were literally 'Living Life in the Fast Lane'. We had exactly twenty minutes to eat lunch. What this meant was that we left the job site at twelve o'clock and had to be back on the job by twelve twenty. Everything was rushed. The good thing was that I loved my job. I was literally the first *woman* welder in all of New England Electric. During that time I learned how to live in the now. I embraced every moment and focused on every second of each thing I was doing. I was never sapped of energy. My energy soared. This is what Eckhart Tolle spoke about when he discussed the Power of Now. For when you focus on what you need to do tomorrow or next month it will certainly drain you. As a welder; I focused on each bead of weld, watching the melting of two metals merge into one. Gliding each welding rod as I led it like a dance over the metal, with my favorite music echoing in the background. Life was complex back then Living life in the fast lane, but there were those moments when I was focused in the now and it was so enlightening. Whenever I focused 100% in something, it showed in my work. I now choose to bring this into my present and future.

When I am in the market I can look at the chicken and thank it for giving its life so I can live. As I'm putting the shopping bags in the car, I am 100% focused on just that. When we lose focus, thinking of what is to come next week, next month... Are you sleeping well? Do you have JOY in your life? Are you thanking your dreams which have come to talk with you to give you guidance or are you rushing about your day? This is where our energy will diminish. Never lose focus of the simple things just because your life becomes complex. Keep it organized. Humans on earth have Free will, but remember the need to micro-manage will drain you. Remember the phase "Let go & Let God". When we partner with God we can let go & enjoy the simple things. Know that God will take care of the details when we walk hand in hand and in alignment with the Universe.

All of the Ascended Masters, Angels and Spirit Guides are here for you as well. But, you must call them. They cannot intercede without your asking them to help. They wait for you to call upon them and give them a job! Tell them what you need, then let go & watch it unfold. Detachment is the key to manifestation. Put your prayers out there and trust that they be done. Love is the Power, Love with all your heart, do not fear. Love is truth. Truth is what you seek. Most of what I am telling you here, you already know. Throughout all of your lifetimes you have gained spiritual growth.

This is just the reminder, the awakening if you will of the light in your DNA. Yes, once scientists thought there was "junk" in our DNA. God didn't make Junk! This unknown piece is actually Light. There are experiments to show how it reacts with Light, sort of like turning it on. Hopefully science will come out with these documents soon.

Shamballa Multidimensional Healing®

Includes Clearings, Meditations, Code activations, DNA clearings and activations. The following is the description for Shamballa Multi-Dimensional Healing class.

The central core of Shamballa is Love—Love and Freedom. Love for oneself and an innate

knowingness of one's connection with Mother/Father God and all Creation. Freedom from

all that stands in the way of that knowingness. Freedom to know who you are, and to step

into your Power, to step into your Mastery. The ascended Master Germain assures us that

the Shamballa energies are now part of an Energetic Grid-work around the Earth.

We may call upon easily at any time.

NOW is the time to release all unnecessary programs from the past and to prepare to receive the new energies coming in. We are about to co-create here on Earth things beyond our imagination. You are invited to be present in each and every moment, and to enjoy the dance through to the end of time.–Hari Babba Melchizedek (John Armitage) & Master Germain.

Shamballa is another form of hands on healing, similar to Reiki but more intense energy. If I was to explain it as color, I would say

Reiki is Red/Orange/yellow and Green. Shamballa is Pink, Violet and Purple. Shamballa is a higher and fine tuned vibration and frequency. This technique comes from St. Germain.

Many years ago in my very first Shamballa class many I connected up, & the light got more intense… it looked like I was in a column, much like the star trek movies where they stand & beam up… in this column a beam of white light filled it, it looked like when you see the sun coming through the window & you can see particles in the air… only these particles were gold speckles & they were moving faster & faster, all the way up to the heavens & deep into the center of the earth, I was in the middle & it was going faster & faster… My Crown chakra was spinning faster & faster & I didn't want it to stop. This began as soon as I grounded the light coming through me to the center of the Earth. It was extremely intense. I kept thinking wow, more! It was so intense. I knew this was what every teacher I have ever had was talking about when they said, connect up & bring in the light… all these years, I thought I knew what they were talking about, but not until that very day when I EXPERIENCED IT ! All these years, I was imagining it… & thought I was doing it right…. Until I experienced it; The Blessed Virgin Mother Mary came to me and showed me details of what I need to do and how to explain it so others could understand. This is where the details came from for the beginning of this book under the chapters of "Connecting with Spirit" and the "Great Central Sun".

Bermuda Triangle

What if you were shown what happens in the Bermuda Triangle?

While waking up one morning, it was that between time where you're not yet awake, and not sleeping either. IT is that between time where you are literally between the worlds. It is here where lucid dreaming takes place. It is here where you ask a question and will be taken to that information which will show you as if in a video, the answer to that question. One Thursday morning I asked "show me about the Bermuda triangle". I had always been curious about the happenings of this location on earth. It seems as if planes and boats seem to disappear without a trace. Some have said that the airplane and vessel control panel instruments go crazy in this area. I was shown this as the gauge indicator was spinning around, completely around. Most gauges needles (indicators) will only go so far and stop; so this in itself was quite abnormal. I was shown an airplane full of people. I could see as if I was up above yet in the cockpit of the plane. The pilot was guiding the plane, co pilot was next to him with a book (some sort of ledger) documenting sequence of events and recording the abnormal activities of the gauges. It started with one, then two, and finally all of them on the dashboard of the plane spun out of control. The plane then ascended up into the clouds as a window seemed to open right there in the middle of the clouds. The clouds became blurry and yet the middle section became clearer and brighter. Once through to the other side the sun got brighter and another 'earth' appeared for them to land on. The plane no longer acted as it did on earth. It seemed to glide instead of fly. The engines were quiet because they had turned off. There was nothing electrical working at all. People were not in a panic. They were relatively calm as if they all knew where they were going and what had just transpired. Their job was done here on earth and they were headed "Home".

Home to the place where they were before they had been born on this planet "Earth". There was no loss, pain or sadness. They behaved as if they were just going to another day at the office. Everything and everyone was calm.

I wondered if they had passed through to another dimension; it certainly seemed as if it could be like that, yet I have nothing to compare it to. When I had previously traveled to dimensions in my mind, it was always a frame of mind that I'd go to; to gather information – for the questions I had. I would be taken to the "temple of wisdom" to find answers to anything I needed. I'd be taken to a temple, but never shown how one could travel in a craft or vessel if you will to get there. I had never seen another globe in the distance to know it was far away from Earth.

This time as the plane traveled through the clouds, my perspective was from up above, high up above because I could see the whole plane and also the globe of another planet it was headed for. The first frame of my witness was in the plane cockpit, then I could see the people in back of the plane from front looking back, then from back looking front as I walked forward.… Then I seemed to have gone through the windshield to take a new position of above the plane as it moved forward and I could then see the globe it was headed for. The globe looked just like earth, with blue waters and swirling cloudy surfaces and also mountainous ranges, plateau's and flat planes (as in the ground not an aircraft).

So what if we really are born into this earth plane of existence without any knowing of where we came from. And What if we came from a place where we actually signed up for a human experience; to learn lessons so our Soul could Jump to the next level in growth? Just as my first Shaman Elder taught me, so many years ago.

It all seemed to make sense on that day. It was the knowing. You know that feeling of knowing? The one where you look at your hand at the end of your arm and know it is yours. Your fingers are moving, and you know you're making them move, yet how is it really happening? Do you think about the tendons and ligaments and the brain signals making your fingers move? No. You just know it.

This witness of the plane going into the next level of existence – Is this the place where we go when a human dies? Back to where they were before birth here on Earth?

It makes so much sense now. I've seen it, I witnessed it with my own eyes, smelled the interior of the plane and even the woman's hair who came close to me during this experience. She had showered using herbal essence shampoo. I am familiar with this scent. As a witness I entered each scene of existence; without a doubt that it was real. For I was there; I saw it with my own eyes.

Once fully awake, I laid in bed thinking. I knew what had just transpired. It was like nothing I had ever experienced before yet

I knew with every morsel of my being what happened, where I was and what I saw. Don't take my word for it... Do your own Google search: Whistleblower Laura Magdalene Eisenhower, Ike's great-granddaughter, outs secret Mars colony project. Then do some research and read everything you can on Robert Dean who was interviewed by www.projectcamelot.org for more interesting information. Pray for Truth and it shall be shown to you. Do not fear, it is just as it should be, all in Divine order with God guiding us.

Another revelation happened when I was shown the "spark of life". This is why scientists were unable to make test tube babies... UNTIL they crashed the atoms (sperm.egg?) with Dolly the Lamb, it worked when the atoms were crashed with ELECTRICITY... which is LIGHT... which is LIGHTENING! Yes, this is it! The spark of Life, is the spark of LIGHT, which is what is in each DNA! There is NO JUNK DNA It is light!

Light is God !

Each night before you retire to bed, ask God to take you to the Temples of Wisdom, the Library of Alexander or a place where you can enhance your spiritual growth and wisdom.

Responsibility

You now have the responsibility to move forward with integrity. You have the ability to get your own answers. You may eventually be helping family, friends and others with your new found intuition. Discretion is a must; just as spoken about in the previous chapters. Discretion must be used in all areas of this work. Imagine if you were reading tarot cards for a friend, and you found cards leading to winning the lottery. Realize that after one receives this information, their future decisions may be influenced by this reading. Imagine a person; thinking they'd soon win the lottery, as they begin spending uncontrollably…

Divination can reveal opportunities. Realize that any time information comes to us, it is only an opportunity. Once the opportunity presents itself, it may or may not be changed.

You have a responsibility to let others know that this information must be understood as an 'opportunity' only. Once the information is out there, it is in your conscious mind yet subconsciously, it *can* change. Your subconscious now has the information and can actually change your path of destiny. Nothing is cut in stone.

My friend Karla intuitively got information that she would be getting a new home. Her focus on the details of this new home was relentless. For the entire six months all she did was talk about this new house. At the same time her husband was training for a promotion at work. The new house Karla thought was to be hers was sold to another family. She was devastated. She asked time after time, how could this be? Her intuition was so accurate for many years; how could this be wrong? A month later, the truth was revealed… Had she not been involved with the idea of a new home coming to her; she would have been on her husband's back trying to make sure he passed the tests for his promotion. You see, Spirit guided Karla (who was a very controlling person) to be preoccupied so her husband could relax to pass the tests. All was in Divine order.

Don't force Spirituality; Pray and it will come naturally. Strive for integrity, impeccability and walk in alignment with Spirit and you are sure to have Fun, Freedom, Joy, Love and Laughter. When you walk in alignment with the Universe/ Creator – God will work on your behalf for your Soul's highest good at all times. Love is the highest vibration of anything on earth. When we bring Love to any situation, we bring Truth, Light and Joy. Life can be better than we have ever dreamed. Go now and become a Co-Creator of your life. It's time to make your Dreams become a reality...

God Bless,

Elizabeth

Question: Mother Mary, what is your message for me today? E.D.

Answer: Things are rapidly changing in your world today. There is much chaos in the world and your healing techniques are needed daily to hold the energy of your loved ones safe. Bless you for all you do for humanity and mother earth. I honor you this day. At this point in time it is necessary for you to review your practices for accuracy and truth. This review will strengthen your connection to God. Are you one who is afraid to use the word God for fear it may offend someone? Do you actually pray before proceeding in your daily work? Do you pray before meditating to make sure your messages are coming from Divine source? We ask you now to look around yourself. Look around at those who have taught you... look around at those who claim to be healers of all kinds. At one point in time, they may have had powers of unusual magnitude. They may have created miracles and you may have also witnessed these healing miracles...

But, at this time, we ask you to look closely, how many of these healers powers lasted more than 10 years? How many of these healers no longer have the healing power?

Yes, this is where we ask you to look this day... see the accuracy of the thread that is missing in these healers. See the missing thread is the "PRAYER". No longer can one teeter totter on the fence, as you say.. No longer can one talk only about doing what makes them happy and forgetting about God. This will no longer be tolerated at this time. The energy of the world is in great change. You are being called on the carpet as they say... called upon this time for accuracy and truth. You will be held accountable. The Shaman must be held accountable for his & her actions. The Shaman who has forgotten how to pray will lose powers within seven to ten years as Dark forces will take over and manipulate. KNOW this now and secure your protection. Return to Prayer, connect with Jeshua, Buddha, Sai Baba and Ascended Masters who have come to help you remember your roll of service on earth. God sent many helpers for you, make sure you are speaking to one sent by God. How to do this? Unequivocally know you are speaking to the right source when you begin Prayer in the name of "Jesus Christ". When you speak in commandments strength comes in... "In the name of Jesus Christ, I command for the Guidance of God and God only, All others, go back where you came from, you cannot use me. God protect me from anyone or anything that would, or could harm me in any way, shape or form, on all levels, planes and dimensions, consciously, unconsciously and subsciously; thank you, it is done, it is done, it is done, so be it, Thy will be done. Call upon Jeshua, the answers will be clear when you are in prayer. Bless you this day. I am Mother Mary

Answer: Many years ago in a workshop in Arizona, the facilitator told me to bury my cross. There in the center of my budding mesa (portable Shamanic Prayer Altar similar to the Native Prayer Bundle) was my cross with Jesus. This woman actually wanted me to bury it in the ground. I refused. She said the cross was reinforcing the horrible things the Catholic church did. I knew MAN changed the church, I also knew MAN, himself, twisted many things that otherwise could have been good with many religions. It was MAN that did this and not what God or Jesus intended it to be. Being raised Catholic; Jesus was a real part of my life. I know to this very day this is because of my connection to Jesus that I am held in the White Light of Christ which keeps me safe each and every day. Thank you and Bless you Jesus. Elizabeth

Greetings Dear Children of the Earth. It is with great pleasure we honor you today. For those of you who are wondering what is this 11-11-11

it is today, November being the 11th month and the 11th day and the 11th year when added 2+0+0+9 = 11. 11 is a master number, meaning it is most powerful. It has been document across the ages that 11:11 is a code that will fire certain codes of consciousness within your brain. On this day, the Portal is open for intense energies of Enlightenment to stream forth from the Heavens to all who desire to work in the Light. This will OPEN your mind for the information of TRUTH to be identified. This will OPEN your Consciousness for the Knowledge of the ancient ones to be identified and come to the surface. This will allow the wisdom of all of your past lives to come forward for healing, and growth. If you recall, there has been several times in the past few years when you looked at the clock and it read 11:11 - at that moment in time, certain neurons fired in your brain to unlock the codes and keys that have been place there from the time you were in Atlantis, Lemuria and the city of MU. These keys and codes are to awaken you to the Ancient Wisdom of all ages; The remembering of everything that ever was and ever will be as listed in the book of Akashic Records. On this day, you have a choice to follow your Soul's path as you have written in your blueprint for life. A choice to accept these Divine Energies of Light & Love. A choice to raise your vibration and follow the path of Light. Today will be a day for you to decide to make a difference. We are the legion of Angels, Ascended Masters, and your Guides, waiting for you to call upon us for guidance.

As with any transition of energy, The influx of Light & Love along with the raising of vibrations can be taxing to the human until the human body becomes comfortable with the new energies... Remember to drink plenty of water, eat as much fresh Organic fruit & vegetables and get plenty of Rest. Spend some time outside in Nature and give thanks to Mother Earth. Live, Love and Laugh as you Go forth in Peace, Love & Light. Blessings to all, Mother Mary

Question: Elizabeth, must someone pray through an intermediary?

Answer: There is only one God; supreme above all. God is not only above us, but around us and in us, thus, our connection with our Soul. We are all connected with God, with the breath within us all. Some call God our Higher Self, Energy, Great Spirit, or Creator. It is all God. It is our higher guidance. Connecting to the creator that gave us the breath of Life is God.

When we command in the name of Jesus, we are commanding that everything Dark Negative or Evil must go, "you cannot use me"... God takes this up to heavens for healing & transformation.

Ascended Masters, Jesus, Mother Mary, Buddah, are our helpers, our brothers & sisters who have gone before us to show us the way.

Mother Mary is partial to Jesus. She tells me to Pray to him, through him & with him daily. Many people need the intermediary because talking directly to or with God seems unattainable. Personally, my connection for guidance is an interactive communication with God with all of God's helpers as my best friends.

Blessings,

Elizabeth

Greetings Dear Children of the Light,

The forces of evil have been at it again as the darkness shadows parts of Mother Earth, Iceland Volcano & Volcanic Ash and the Oil spill in the Gulf have been wreaking havoc on earth and its inhabitants. Since the beginning of time the battle between Dark and Light has gone on.

During this day and age, it is important to know which side you are on, there is no more teeter-tottering on the fence' as you say. You must choose and be prepared to be called to action at any time. You must be responsible for your thoughts, words and Actions.

The World is your home. You have been called forth to protect not only yourself, your family and friends; but also your neighbor, your neighbors family and friends with LOVE in your heart as you have for your own.

It is said 'all is in Divine order, just as it should be'. These words should not be construed to mean you do nothing. APATHY will not be tolerated; as you sit and watch others suffer. If there is so much as a thread of help you can offer you are asked to be called into action to do so. Holding the vision (of what you wish) is not enough.

As a Light-worker, Shaman, Medicine person; you say holding the vision for (positive results) is a must - yes, this is very powerful, but only when you ADD POSITIVE ACTION.

It is true, your thoughts, words, emotions and action is God's Way. You will be rewarded a million fold... Prayer, Vision, Good Thoughts, with Good Emotions followed through with an act of kindness and Love is what I ask of you from this moment forward. Take heed of these words now and go forth in action with Love... Jeshua.

If you have extra food... invite your neighbor who may have lost his/her job... Elizabeth

Once upon a time you were a different person, much different than you are today. You may have been that "Material" person; with the only focus of who said what at the company picnic. The common phone call consisted of the juiciest gossip of the day. Having drinks with friends, making small talk often judging those around you. What else was there to do? It was a habit. You never gave it a bit of thought. You never thought your words could damage anyone. It was harmless gossip. Or so you thought. You didn't know that jealousy can actually tear a rip in someone's aura. (The energy field surrounding a person)

As you grew, your life changed. You learned about the Law of Attraction – what you vibrate in you attract. Like attracts like, and most of all how your emotions vibrating in anger could indeed attract more anger towards you. Yes, now at this time of your life, Science has actually proven the Metaphysical "New Age" subjects. Science has proven that human beings emit a vibration that can be measured (frequency) and more tests are being done to prove even more of the once called 'wishy washy' subjects.

Did you know that when your thoughts, words and emotions are congruent (equal); that is the key to manifesting; Manifesting your heart's desire.

Think about this for a moment. Before you get into your car, you think of getting in the car. Before you put the key in the ignition, you think 'put the key in the ignition'. This is done subconsciously. Thoughts are extremely powerful in manifesting anything.

When you speak, you are putting a vibration to your thoughts. Hold your hand over your throat and speak… you can feel vibrations of your vocal chords on your hand. These vibrations are sent out with each spoken word all to hear… These vibrations are sent into the "ethers" (the air/atmosphere/Heaven). Emotions added to Thoughts and spoken words amplify the intent.

In order to manifest: one must have their thoughts, words and emotions all on the same exact line of intent… They must all be congruent.

If you think 'this job stinks'; then speak "I hate my job"; and when you wake up in the morning, you have the feeling of 'ugh! I don't want to go to work'… Sooner or later, you'll either loose that job, or attract more negativity surrounding it. (You could actually even attract an accident surrounding the job). You absolutely cannot have a wonderful job with these types of thoughts, words and emotions.

One day you will find a topic of discussion that makes you feel good. Notice the type of positive words you speak about it along with the positive thoughts you're thinking. Notice how good you feel. This is how you manifest… Capture that feeling. Recognize the Positive Words around the subject and then identify the positive thoughts surrounding it.

The key here is to control your thoughts. If you could control your every thought, you would then manifest all positive things. And attract more Positive results in every way.

Some humans think thoughts are random and there is no controlling them. This is not true. You have choices. When someone cuts' you off on the highway, you can think, 'Wow, what a jerk…' or you can think 'I sure hope they are not rushing to an accident/ problem/ or have a sick child'. There are many choices for everything you think, do and say.

If you look at each individual on earth when they've done something you think was wrong; and think "I wonder what their path is in this life" "I wonder what blueprint they came in with and what plan they are following". You would soon realize that when you judge another person's motives you may be way off! God only knows why that person did what they did. Or why they acted in that manner. There was once a common phrase "you don't know another man until you've walked in his shoes". There is much truth to those old wives tales and phrases. Pay attention to them and you will learn much.

You can never change another person… BUT you can make subtle changes in yourself that makes that person WANT to change. Stop doing the dance – Action/ RE-action. Stop it. Ok, here's the scenario – you've come home from a long, hard day at work. Your spouse begins to nag at you. You begin to react; you spouse gets louder because you're not 'hearing' what is said… you react again with more harboring words. It magnifies into something you later wish had not happened. No one wins. If you could enter that scenario with different ideas; the idea 'you are not going to do that dance again' may yield different results, put a little compassion in your heart.

Here's an example. Jane is always late for family events. Her husband Dick spends endless hours trying to make her conform to being on time. By the time they arrive, the holiday dinner is cold, the rest of the family is cleaning up and it's obvious they've been fighting all the way. For 20 years; same scenario, same dance. Until one day Dick decided he was not going to do this anymore. He jumped into a car with other family members and arrived at the wedding on time, leaving Jane to fend for herself. It took a few dinner engagements; but sooner or later Jane realized if she didn't hurry up, she was going to be left behind. The situation was not working for Jane any longer and she had to make changes. Remember, you cannot change another person; but *you can, make subtle changes in yourself that make the other person want to change.*

In Love, and Light, Kateri Tekakwitha

Dear Children of the Light,

It is I; ORYON speaking to you now through the host in which you refer to as Elizabeth. She has asked of me today if we have a message for humanity. We do. Thus in times of great changes, we are honored to be asked for our words of wisdom. We recommend that you always use your guidance of the highest source. Truth is coming to the forefront but has not yet emerged among the masses in full forces as yet. There are those still continuing to deceive. Unbeknownst to them, the Karma they will incur will be unbearable. They would be wise to double think their actions of such magnitude. There are also those who are backed by dark forces. You know who they are. You can sense it. It is those times when you know things are just not right. We ask you to call in the highest of the high to deal with such, for unless you have been trained and prepared to transmute such negativity it would be to your advantage to call in Archangel Michael and his Sword of Blue Flame or St. Germain for the Violet Flame – the Fire of Transmutation to transform these harmful energies with Love and Light back to God.

It is the Law of Physics that states energy cannot be created nor destroyed; it can only change state. For example, a solid can change into liquid, and then into a gas by applying heat. This is law. Negative Energies can be transmuted by using the Violet flame of St. Germain. This Violet flame is similar to the Welder's torch; it must have the perfect mix of Oxygen & Acetylene (Gas) in order to obtain the perfect violet/blue flame. When this flame is perfect; nothing can pass through this flame without changing state. If it is a solid, it will turn to liquid, if it is liquid, it will become a gas. When you call upon St. Germain to transmute negative energies with this Violet flame;

those harmful negative energies will change state & be taken to the Light for healing & transformation with Love.

Through your determination, you have gained instruction which has raised you to this level among the hierarchy of what you call life. Life with its many lessons; is the ladder to success. But now you're learning differently, you feel something has changed. Success as you once thought was the social status of society. You have now begun to understand that is no longer the way. That old way of thinking, was the "Material" world. The Material world, fed by Ego was all you knew. Everyone worked hard to obtain the 'toys' necessary to "have fun" as you say... until one day, that feeling of 'wow' you got when you sat in that new car, just didn't do it anymore. One day, the excitement was gone. Something was missing, and you just couldn't identify it. Your search in every aspect of pleasure resulted in more searching, until one day... Was it a near death experience? An illness? Or was it meeting someone who was enlightened? They radiated Peace, Joy, Love, and Light? What was that Light? They seemed to beam with Light, emanating from every cell of their being. When they spoke with you, something touched your heart. It made your crown chakra spin. It felt good. At first you didn't know what this was. You only knew that you wanted more of it.

Thus began the touch of Spirituality. A touch of God is what happened. It woke up the God within you and you wanted more. How do you get more? Meditation? Prayer? Workshop with Spiritual people? Time alone walking in the woods? At the beach? In the Mountains? As you have found, once you ignited this spark of God within you, the inspiration became glorious. It was like finding home after years of being away. This connection with God has ignited the life force within you. You have now a glimpse of what being a "co-creator" of life is all about. Walking hand in hand with God, your Creator every day in every way. Follow your heart for it warms the soul. It is the Joy within you that will reinforce your intuition to let you know you are on the right path. When you are on the right path, you are walking in alignment with the Universe (Creator/God). When you are walking in alignment with God; Doors will open for you that you never thought possible. Opportunities will come in places unforeseen. This is what is meant by Co-Creation. You can make your dreams become a reality.

Whatever you choose to do; do it 100% with Love in your heart. Your generation has found a new way of doing things called 'multi-tasking'. This is harmful to your energy fields. Let me explain. You are trying to accomplish more than one thing at the same time; because you say you don't have time. Each task has not been tended to with 100% of your attention. It has also been accomplished without Love in your heart. Then you wonder why you are drained and exhausted at the end of the day.

When you tend to each task with focus on that one task, and see/ hear/ feel or imagine that it is the one and only task you have for the day, and approach it with Love in your heart... That task will reap rewards exponentially. Amazingly you will find, that it has been accomplished in such a short amount of time, that it was as if time stood still. When you focus on the one task at hand, (one at a time) with Love in your heart not only will the job be done to perfection, but your energy will soar and your Soul will illuminate...

Blessings in Love and Light.

ORYON

Note: Oryon comes from the of stars now known as the constellation of Orion

Orion's Belt can be seen as the 3 bright stars in a row that are visible throughout the world in the night sky.

Greetings Dear Children of the Light,

As many things come to our attention we feel the need to share our thoughts with those who wish to improve their Spiritual Paths.

Spiritual Awakening can put one on the fast track to remembering... You're not learning because you have done this many times before;

you are remembering that which you had forgotten. You are awakening with every cell of your body. You are remembering every lifetime you've had and where you were when you lived it. You were with us in the City of Atlantis, the City of Lemuria and the City of Mu. You buried crystals of knowledge to find in this lifetime for you to remember the wisdom of all ages. This explains the fascination you have now with crystals and gems of the earth. Many of you have had such Spiritual awakening and are working ever so hard to recall all of the wisdom you had. The only problem with this is also that many of you are getting burned out. You are doing too much too soon without working on yourself to repair the stress, energy shifts and losses of each day. You have awakened to the Spiritual understanding that you have a special purpose of Life here on earth. You are a Light-worker. You are working with and on many people, helping the masses in many ways. However, you are not tending to yourself. This is detrimental to your physical health. Many of you have developed physical ailments. Many of you have reached a point of burn out. Some of you are even questioning if you want to continue this path. We ask you now to heed these words.

It would be to your benefit to seek a Spiritual partner of higher integrity to work on your physical body. Many of the Healing modalities will help you to maintain a higher state of energetic perfection. Choose one that calls to you. Cranial Sacral, Shiatsu', Reiki, Shamballa, Reflexology, there are many. This will solidify your aura to prevent rips and tears. This will help maintain your highest state of energy to enable you to be the best you can be to hold the highest amount of Light possible. It is imperative that you dowse it out (verify with your intuition)/ go with your inner gut feelings of higher intuition before selecting a practitioner to work with or on you. This is absolutely imperative.

If you wish, we can show you how many times a practitioner with ego, actually dumps negativity onto the client. We work to guide you on many levels, this energy exchange of heaviness that comes in your blueprint; for you to learn discernment, and demand higher forms of energy in Love and Light. Refuse to work with anything less than the best. It is to your advantage to understand your own answers. Do not visit a practitioner just because she/he is highly recommended. For your highest good; you must ask if it is in your Highest and Best interest before making such appointments.

When you were in grade school, you were taught many things; the simple things of life and how to live on Earth. As you graduated into higher forms of education, some of the simple things of years ago became lost. The same is true for all forms of learning. How many of you forget the simple teachings from the beginning of your Spiritual path? How many of you forget to clean your living spaces? Do you think it is fine to be a healer and yet, not be diligent in Feng Shui for your own home/lives? How many healers are broke? How many healers are hurt? How many have home lives of chaos? How many have non supportive families? As you walk your talk, things will begin to fall into place.

As you study with many teachers throughout your life; I remind you here to "take the good stuff, and leave the crap behind" as our host, Elizabeth says... This is not our recommended way of speaking such slang, however, the concept is very important. Forget that which does not serve you and blossom only GOOD seeds of knowledge from each teacher into plants of Wise Wisdom. Don Manuel would say, "if you can't grow corn with it..." (leave it behind). The end results of your studies will percolate into Enlightenment: 'Wise words of Wisdom of Truth, Integrity and Impeccability with Unconditional Love for All'.

I remind you now to look into the very first teachings from all of your teachers... go through you notes. Find the little holes in your work, the areas you have neglected... Remember to keep only the good... leaving that which does not serve you. Patch up the holes; by walking your talk. Are you teaching? Are you meticulous in what you teach? Or are you one who teaches as if it is a fairy book story, yet you are not living the story? (We won't even go into teaching only for the money... that would be a slap to your face. We know you know the obvious… We are here reminding you of the forgotten manicuring little details to sterilize your Spiritual lives).

You have witnessed what we call the Weekend Shaman. Those who practice Shamanic techniques only with people who "believe" in what they do. (This is true for all Spiritual Healers, not just Shamans). Do you realize, when YOU believe in what you do… Others' will follow.

Does a Doctor wait for a patient to believe in him? Or does the Doctor just do his work with confidence…. Because he knows he has been properly educated, he has obtained what is necessary to graduate and he follows through by going to work each day… This is the similarity I wish to bring to you this day… As a Healer, you must believe / KNOW your own work inside and out. You must KNOW you have a solid connection to /with God without a morsel of doubt. You must know that God will work to protect you every step of the way.

We understand it takes many of your earth years to understand this concept. Until then, continue your daily rituals for Protection. You have many rituals and prayers. It is the prayers that you know in your heart, without a doubt are solid, that will provide the most solid protection. One day, without a doubt… you will know your connection to God is solid, and you will no longer need outside rules, rituals or tools for protection. Until then, use what you feel is necessary. Aim for Truth, Impeccability and Integrity with Love in your heart for everything you think, do and say.

Don Manuel taught in his class before he crossed over and continues to teach from the Spirit world- The Shamans Covenant with God: "When I call, God answers… When God Calls… I SAY YES!" without hesitation…

Healers' maintenance is a must.

Would you purchase a car and never maintain it? Why would you not care for your physical body? Make sure nutrients are most excellent and closest to their natural form. A vitamin/mineral that is not absorbed into the body is only wasted. Be conscientious with your nutrition. Do your home-work, never take another's words as gospel. Always search for Truth and accuracy in all things.

At this time we would like to address Reiki – Just a note here. To remind you to work only with those with no less than 75% Light; always. What is meant here is the fact that as Reiki was re-introduced into your culture, there are some who neglected to bring God into this work. This is why there has been much controversy over this healing modality. Some are teaching Reiki and stating, connect with whatever you want... this is not a religion. However, although this is true, Reiki is not a religion, it must be taught with the connection coming from the Life force of the Universe... GOD. The same God, that gave you the spark of life. The One and Only Supreme energy being; God. Remember this always. Bring God into everything you think, do and say and you will always be protected. Opportunities will present themselves in extraordinary ways.

So, by now, you may have noticed ringing in your ears, light headed, vibrations in certain parts of your body (sometimes just a foot, or hand, other times your whole body), flashes of light, and maybe even symbols flashing before your eyes; hot flashes, headaches and dizziness. You may be experiencing one or many of these symptoms. They are adjustments being done to your physical body in preparation for ascension into the 5th Dimension. You now live on earth in what you call the 3rd dimension – this is only one of many Planes, Levels and Dimensions that exist. This Ascension is not what you would refer to as dying. It is the raising of your vibrations to hold the maximum amount of Light. To fulfill your Divine purpose and work with the company of Heavens again; along side your brothers and sisters of the Light you now call Ascended Masters, Angels and Saints. This will truly become Heaven on Earth as the Ancient ones spoke of many years ago.

You have free will. It is law. Although you have selected a Divine blueprint for this lifetime, you have free will which will allow you to choose to follow this Divine plan or not. The Heavens will not think less of you if you choose to rest in this life. We love you always. Oryon.

Greetings Dear Children,

I call you children even though you are of all ages from infant to elderly; it matters not. What matters is the understanding that age has no difference. Your Souls are timeless; living and having lived through many lifetimes and will move on to living in more lifetimes to come.

I am called here today to speak to you now about a subject that has taken off on your planet. Yes, taken off in many directions, good, bad, ugly, fearful, excited… What is this 2012, what is ascension? Most reference books speak of Ascension as the rising of Christ from Earth to Heaven. Some people welcome Ascension with bliss and others hear the word and panic. In some religions it is referred to (ascension) as something that happens 'after' you die. So in the Earthly concept; why would anyone want to ascend? For on your earth, the desire is to live life, and continue to avoid death at any cost. (You can see this by what people do in medical fields to preserve life). Many on earth do not understand that your Soul is eternal. As an Energy that cannot be created nor destroyed; the Soul changes form when the time in the physical body has been completed. The Soul moves through the dimensions to another which is appropriate at that time.

As we have spoken here before about energy, Light, and Love, we will stress upon the important points at this time to help prepare you for the bombardment of negative energies that you encounter each and every day. It is imperative that you flood your chakras with the White Light of Christ each and every day; this is your feeding tube from Creator God. This White Light of Christ will not only feed you, but it will protect you from that which can harm you un-necessarily. Is there necessary harm; you ask… Yes, there are some harmful things you have, what you call, 'signed up for' in this life, to present those lessons necessary for you to Learn, or how you say, to get your Soul to grow to the next level in Spiritual Growth. Each and every illness, injury and occurrence in our life was placed there before you were born into this world. Your energy field contains a blueprint of your life; of such occurrences to take place for your Soul to move up the stairway to hierarchy.

Most important at this time is to control the emotions; because they can take over and spiral you into a chaotic spin of negativity. When you notice an emotion other than LOVE coming into your presence, it is wise to acknowledge it and ask why this is here. Emotions are only a reaction to someone or something. Emotions are not tangible; and therefore, you have choices. You choose to have an emotion based upon your past. Your past experience will determine how you react to such occurrences and which emotion you choose. At the point of time where you feel an emotion showing itself as "fear"; take the time to assess the situation. There are those times when fear is needed for example; to catapult your-self into the fight or flight mode and run out of a burning house. However, there are also those times when fear creeps up and inhibits productivity. Fear can prevent you from moving forward in a positive manner. When you have assessed the situation and there is no present need for fear; we ask you to question thoroughly if, when, why, how and where the fear is. Ask these questions with LOVE in your heart. Know that you are a Divine Being of Love and Light. Creator God put you here on Earth with your co-operation. You choose this life and everything in it. Question as you would speak face to face with an innocent child you love... We ask you to do this first because we realize it is most difficult for many of you to know you are speaking to God. We realize it is most difficult for many of you to know you ARE God. So we will begin here with questioning the Loving child...

At this time we ask you to see, feel, or imagine you are questioning fear as if you were speaking directly your Loving Child; because this is so. And then when you are comfortable with that we ask you to go inside yourself, and question yourself, as GOD... Because you are connected to the All ONE... We are ALL ONE... You will know that YOU Are God, God is You and you Are One with All of Creation. No different than the Tree, the rock, the bird and your brother.

As energy beings we have vibrations. Fear is a lower form of vibration. Once the fear is questioned, this questioning process will immediately raise your lower vibrations of fear up to a higher level. As Elizabeth says; "up a notch". (We chuckle at her metaphoric use). During this time where much consciousness has been in 2012 mode; we suggest this questioning of fear as most important at this time. People have spoken of 2012 with negativity such as: "The world will end", "ET's will come", and most locally here in this state… it has even been said "Rhode Island will be under water". There have been Maps printed showing which states will no longer be (in the USA); as if they have disappeared or been submerged under water. There has also been much prophesized in this area from the Hopi, the Maya and other indigenous tribes. The Mayan Calendar has been said to END on Dec 21, 2012.

My Dear Children do you know that Negative forces FEED on Negative energies? Yes, Negative, Dark energies FEED on FEAR, Anger, Depression, Hate, and all of the lower energies.

Energy attracts more of the same energy… Like attracts like. Negative energy attracts more negative energy. The quickest way to raise out of the negative energy vibrations is to think/ be/ feel LOVE. LOVE is the Highest of all energy on Earth. Pure Unconditional Love will combat all forms of negativity. So you ask, when you are emotionally trapped into a state of anger/hate/fear and depression, how can you get into that feeling of Love? Carry a picture of your most treasured and loved friend/ child/ puppy/ place or thing… Remember the day you first laid eyes on your very own baby? Remember the very first time you took a moment to watch the sun rise with your true love? Remember being held in your mother's arms… whatever scenario will help you to remember the feeling of true Unconditional Love… Capture this in a memory now and save it in your wallet for a time when you need to recall it.

2012 will come and what you will see will be the raising of consciousness like never before. What we mean by this is the fact that… 20 years ago you would have not been speaking of such things as Ascension, Light and Love. You have witnessed the opening of the minds for many to begin to grasp the knowledge that there is more to the physical body, and as more than the physical body, we are all connected. We are all connected to the ONE Creator God of all things. These concepts are some of the wisdom of the ages coming to the forefront. This is known as the Awakening. More of this will come. Truth will not be denied. Government, religion and corporate systems will no longer be able to lie to the public. All will come forward in truth. Little by little it began and now you have seen more and more of this has already begun to happen. No longer will Earth be a place of every man for himself. The consciousness will be for the good of all with every man looking out for his and her brother. Peace will no longer be an idea; but will be demanded from every nation worldwide. Heaven on earth will no longer be a dream; but a reality.

Remember there is nothing here on earth that you have not signed up for... When God brings you to it… God will bring you through it. We are your brother and sisters in the Light. As you may have already witnessed, time is speeding up. Things are changing and you may need extra help to get through this with grace and ease. It is wise for you to also call upon your earth brothers and sisters who have been trained in Healing arts. It is wise to know where to go to raise your education and where to go to heal your-self. Elizabeth has now been guided to hold individual training and healing sessions through the newest technology you call 'Skype'. Through this Skype session with the accompaniment of video technology; Energy can be shifted, knowledge can be guided into Wisdom, and it is no longer necessary to travel long distance for the Masters training. Many of you have studied with masters, yet after your week long training the master is no longer assessable to you for every day questions. We have sent Elizabeth to study with 26 Master Shamans (Medicine Men and Women) from all over the world. She has traveled through the dimensions working with Ascended Masters; training with the Keys and Codes to unlock Karma of the Past, Present and Future. She has been groomed for healing earthly situations and has a direct connection to us in the White Light of Christ; in God; with Unconditional Love. We thank you for your time to listen to our message this day. For we are your brothers and sisters in the light. Although I am Jesus speaking, this day I speak for all of Ascended Masters of Love and Light.

Blessings to you with Love.

I Am You, You Are Me, We are ALL One with GOD.

Jeshua

Greetings dear Children of the Light,

We hear your calling. We hear you plea for peace, for danger to stop lerking upon the earth and the chaos and pain that has come. We know itis difficult to understand but Please, please try to understand that all is in Divine order. Know that upon death all pain and karma is released to the Light. Earth; your school is only temporary. Your human body is only temporary, for you are more than your physical body, you are eternal energy - a soul; A member of God's family of Light. When earth life becomes difficult, call upon any of us (Ascended Masters, Angels of Love and Light, Buddha, Quan Yin, Jesus, Mother Mary & Joseph, Saint Germain, Hilarion, El Morya, Kuthumi and myself - Oryon. We are all messengers of God. We are here for you. We will bring you strength you need to carry on. We will help to guide you to safey and Light. All you have to do is ask. Call our name out loud, or in your mind... For we hear your every thought. We come to protect you for those of you who have choosen the difficult path of this lesson plan on earth... We will help you to be strong so you can endure that which you have to accomplish here on earth. Remember us, for we are there for you every moment of every day. Blessings of Love – Oryon

Things to ponder upon to help raise your consciousness:

There is NO such thing as Bad Luck... You choose this life and everything in it before you were born. Yes, You. With the Holy Spirit, Kryon, Angels, Saints, and God you sat among the Masters in the Hall of records - (Akashic Records) before you were born. The recordings of everything that ever was and will be; you were discussing your next role on Earth. This blueprint you formulated at that time was a map to accompany you to Earth... to increase your vibrations... for your Soul to Jump to the next level in Spiritual Growth. For this is the game of Life. Although each of you hold this map; you also have free will when you follow your Earth's mission. You have the choice to ignore your blueprint, and skate free (as you say) to take it easy and rest. Knowing full well, this would cause you to come back to earth in another life to then fulfill your blueprint. The choice is yours. We will not think less of you if you elect a "rest" period of time. We honor you for those lifetimes that you have progressed, to your highest level in Spiritual Consciousness. Each lifetime is a higher level with more 'tests' to be passed. Once the lesson is learned, the test no longer needs to present itself. This is obvious; as you can see with friends who continue to make the same mistakes over and over again... they will continue this cycle until their test has been mastered.

When you meditate, you can understand all of the rules. These rules are often called the "Laws of the Universe". Most people now understand the "Law of Attraction" for it has been written and spoken about in many arenas on earth. There are a series of Laws for your Universe, and it would be to your benefit to study them. Many of you have said "Life doesn't come with a manual". No, it didn't but you have the tools to help you find these "rules" to make the game of life simple and rewarding.

We understand there are many who are bitter for the revealing that the Bible as you know it, has been Re-Written many, many times. This angered many of you. We understand this. Continue on in your search for Truth and Integrity. When you Anger, this makes the emotions in you arise so when you take action - you then have the force behind you to search for Truth. This is actually the ONLY time when anger is a good thing... When you immediately turn it into an ACTION to search for TRUTH... Many of you can now see and feel the people on earth searching for Truth in many arenas; not settling for less than TRUTH. We honor you for this. We bless you for your Perseverance, Commitment, Dedication and Truth.

If you wish to view your Akashic records, you may call upon me for this. When you retire at the end of the day; surround yourself with the White Light of Chirst using the visualization for Christ's Light coming from the Heavens, pouring through your crown chakra, and filling your entire body, coming out your feet, and going deep into the Center of Mother Earth- see/feel or imagine this light *as seen around Jesus' head – called his Halo – fill yourself up and surround yourself with the overflow of this beautiful energy... Anchor it into the Center of Mother Earth as you begin to feel or imagine the continuous flow. Then call to me by invoking my name three times in sequence out loud. El Morya is pronounced (El-Mor-EE-a). Ask for me to accompany you for witness of your Akashic Records. When this mission has been completed to your satisfaction, a simple Thank you will suffice. I leave you now to ponder upon what has been said here. God Bless you in Jesus' name. El Morya.

Greetings Dear children of the Light,

We thank you for your prayers and well wishes for our brothers and sisters in Peru who have witnessed the horrific results of heavy energies... It is because of your prayers that many lives were spared. The planet has erupting in many places, and more of the same has been predicted by many. We tell you now, not to worry. If you worry, then it is only a waste of time. Use your time wisely. Pray to see the world the way you dream it to be... Hold that vision of perfectness, with Unconditional Love and Peace for all. Those high vibrations held by many are what will help to change the future and protect your planet. Then live your life in Joy.

Today we have written some tidbits of information to make you think... for when you use your brain to the max, then and only then will it respond to give you the maximum wisdom. Remember to learn as much as you can to turn knowledge into Wisdom. Remember A.Villoldo wrote: 'knowledge is knowing that water is H2O; Wisdom, is knowing how to make it rain'.

The first tidbit is… "If you do nothing, you are part of the problem". This sentence was given to our host Elizabeth by Don Manuel Quispe in meditation last month. Don Manuel elaborated… There are many who study Spirituality, learn to meditate, think the right thoughts, learn many good things… then do nothing.

How is "nothing" helping humanity? Are these people just living in the bliss of the high states of consciousness? This you call (energy sucker)… Hmmm makes you think now, doesn't it? Give serious thought to your contribution to Earth and its inhabitants.

Of course we still Love you if you do nothing… However… Make sure you are comfortable with your choices, so no Karma accrues. You must be comfortable, in Love and Light with your actions, or non actions… We will not lecture on the following tidbits… they are for you to ponder upon… Use your brain.

Read each one of the following and stop for a moment to think…

…A man of quality cannot be intimidated by a woman of equality.

…When your thoughts, words and emotions are all congruent… then and only then will you manifest your hearts desires with the deepest abundance…

…Emotions are like drinking and driving… Remove emotions and your decisions will be accurate.

…When will people learn that they can't lie to a Light Worker… They are transparent… the light worker sees all… The Light Worker with integrity will walk away and pray for the liar.

…Can you look your enemy in the eye and say "I love you", and mean it?

...Can you hear that your enemy has paid a Shaman to bind you to harm, and still send prayers of Love?

...Can you find your credit card stolen and charged to the max? And be okay with that? And think she must have been really desperate... let me send prayers and love???

A light worker knows that he has put the enemy in his life, for lessons to be achieved, for his soul's growth... A Light worker knows even the "bad guy" has a Soul and is one with all.

...Can you say 'thank you; to your enemy... for the lessons he taught you...?

You must think, speak and feel one with God/ One with All of Creation in order to be at such peace, unconditional love and Light. A state of true humbleness... True enlightenment; is where you are headed... The higher states of consciousness, the fifth dimension of Love and Light awaits you.

...A Light worker has no enemies in this world or the next... A Light worker loves all... unconditionally and knows all is in Divine Order, just as it should be.

Sometimes words are not necessary, just being in the presence of God is all that's needed. Feel the presence, Feel the Love, Feel the warmth of the energy that feeds the entire essence of your being. Feel the Light that permeates every cell of your body, your DNA activating with Light as it feeds your Soul. See/feel or imagine the White Light of Chirst coming from the heavens (the Great Central Sun) up above, way beyond the milkey way... funnel it into your crown chakra and fill every morsel of your body, mind, Spirit & Soul... push it out 10, 12, ... 20 feet around you in all directions, pouring into you and coming out your feet, anchoring into the center of Mother Earth, see the spark of light in the center of Earth, and anchor it there... As this light flows through you, it feeds you; pushing out anything dark, negative or evil and fills it with White Light... Remember, where there is Light, nothing dark negative or evil can exist. Fill yourself with this Light daily; this Light will nurture you, feed you, and protect you in every way, shape and form, on all levels, planes and dimensions... consciously, unconsciously, and subconsciously... always.

Bless you for all you do, we thank you for taking your turn to return to earth to be of service. We wait for your instructions. Tell us what you need, Tell us what you want. Do you need a spiritual adivisor? Do you need a spiritual nutritionist? A spiritual financial advisor? A spiritual fitness coordinator? Many of us were once on Earth in human form as you are now. We know your lives and what is beyond. We have the wisdom of what was, what is, and what will be. We; the Ascended Masters, Angels, Saints, and Spirit Guides of the Light are here for you. We cannot interfere in your life. We must be asked. All you have to do is call upon us... We are waiting. We are your brothers and sisters of the Light. I speak for all of us here and now, with Many many thanks. We Love You, Always, Oryon.

Greetings Dear Children of the Light,

Oryon here again, to discuss electronics not cooperating with Light-workers energy... Oh, yet, but you laugh. For it is true, you know this well. How many times during the past years have you lost computer data? How many times as you say - you have fried - such equipment? Your energy has changed as your vibrations have been raised to harness the energy of such times of enlightenment. Electronics goes poof! Yes, but there is more to this...

Spirit is cleaning out your life. Keeping the good and eliminating that which no longer serves you. As Shaman Teacher Don Manuel would often ask - can you grow corn with it? Meaning - if you cannot make practical use out of it; it is of NO use - discard it.

So it's great if you can meditate, yet if you do not bring back useful information on this third dimension you call Earth, then you are wasting time and energy not serving you, Humanity or Earth. And of course then, what are you doing on Earth, if you are not here to help??? Don Manuel has contacted our host most recently and stated:

"if you do nothing; you are part of the problem! You promised to teach; to keep our lineage and teachings Sacred." Thus with our Host, Elizabeth... We have much to teach, and with her physical presence on Earth in agreement to bring our words to you; this channel is open.

Don Manuel is with us here in Spirit; a wealth of information from the Mountains (Apus) to the Stars (Chaskas). We honor all of you who have spent time with him and hold his teachings sacred. He asks that we remind you to call upon him for his wisdom.

Time is speeding up. What was once taught in a two year program was good for those times... The world needs healers, and NEEDS HEALERS NOW! As time is speeding up; many are teaching a two year program in less time, this is accurate. When information is presented with Integrity, Unconditional Love and Truth; the Student will take less time to digest and percolate knowledge into wisdom because they are Guided in the Light.

As you prepare for bed each night; call upon your guides of Light to bring you to the Temples of Wisdom and Truth. These nightly sessions will reinforce your daily activities with accuracy. If you wish to consciously remember each nightly session, program a Crystal Glass of water: Fill a Crystal Glass of water, pray over it with the intent to remember your dreams upon waking... drink some of the water... (have notebook & Pen at bedside) upon waking drink the rest of the water and write any thoughts that come to mind...

It is time now to take Spiritual inventory of your life. KNOW exactly what you like, and dislike. Speak of only your likes, and wants in order to attract only that which is positive for your life. Totally eliminate dislikes and negative words from your vocabulary... this will help build total co-creation to manifest your desires. -yes we speak of this often, to drill it into your consciousness -

You say, life didn't come with a manual... Life is difficult - yet we are giving you the tools to co-create as you desire... Listen dear one, Understand how important your THOUGHTS, WORDS AND

ACTIONS (emotions) are for manifesting exactly what you think, speak and do... Once again as you say - just for the record - when all three of those highlighted words are in order - then you will manifest exactly what you think, say and feel... it will come to fruition. When you harness this - You will witness how easy it will be to bring good things to life...

In your generations, you have become accustom to much technology which makes your life easy. You are able to do more in less time than your ancestors could. In essence this was an accomplishment. However, now is the time to NOT take advantage of such technology. DO NOT rely solely upon such -short cuts- for you will surely be fried yourself. One day will come when Electronics will not work - We assure you it is in your best interest to back up - as you say - your data - on hard copy; old fashioned paper with pen. This will assure your safe keeping for a lifetime. Documents of days gone by have been preserved for centuries... this is best for preservation.

We Love you Always, Oryon

2010. For eons people spoke about the times to come. They are here. The new energies are here. The Energy Shifts have come. The vibrations are being raised daily and you are learning much. You are embracing these vibrations with Grace and Ease. You are all Children of God. Bless you.

There is nothing to fear. You have been prepared for lifetimes. You are on Earth Not only to learn lessons for your Soul's growth but to have your guiding force be JOY. Yes, Joy. Joy will let you know when you are on your path. When you feel Joy in Prayer, have no doubt that you are in pure guidance. You are here to have fun and enjoy.

Time as you know it has changed. You have witnessed 'time speeding up'. Is it not true that you have not been able to accomplish the same task in the same amount of time as you have in the past??? Synchronicity? Yes, you have witnessed the sequence of events unfolding in miraculous ways. This is your co-creation we spoke about. When your thoughts, words and emotions (actions) are congruent… you are co-creating, manifesting if you will – hour by hour, day by day – it has been spoken before and now you have proof. Science has proven much of what has been spoken in metaphysical circles of years past. One of such is Prayer – Dr. Masato Emoto has proven that Prayer does indeed affect the molecules of water in his many experiments. Do you realize that when you Pray over your food, you will never have food poisoning? Give Thanks for your food, for it giving life, so you may live. This not only refers to meat, but also plants… You do know that each plant/vegetable/ and animal also has the same amount of life force from God. For you vegetarians who will not eat meat, because it is alive … You should know, the Plant is also alive… little humor here… We also like to have fun. We know that you know what we are speaking of here now.

At this time we would like to address a bit more of a delicate nature. We wish to remind you all to walk your talk, and talk your walk. Write this on your mirror and read it to yourself each and every day. We cannot stress this enough. Respect… Integrity… honesty… Impeccability… most important. As time is speeding up, so does your Karma. Once upon a time, as you say, you could talk about someone, and the "stuff" didn't come back to you for a few years. Then as time sped up, it came back in a month… Now you will soon see, if you talk negative about someone, it most certainly will come back to bite you within one hour! Be diligent with your integrity. You can't afford not to. You know this; we are here to remind you…

Embrace your family, Embrace your friends, Embrace their differences and rejoice in the power of knowing that you can accept each and every one with Love despite their annoyance in your life. You have risen above the egotistical annoyance. You can now look at each individual and know they are riding this lifetime along their own path for their own soul's growth. No matter how difficult it is, no matter how difficult they seem to be, the window of opportunity has given you choices. You my friend have chosen the good ones. Not everyone will; and you have to be okay with this. Maybe this is the lifetime they are to 'tread water' and just float around without direction? Maybe this is their lifetime they will be the problem, and not the solution.

Remember that time in Heaven when God was asking for someone to come to Earth to be the "Bad guy"? None of you choose that part. It was father Joe, the greatest disciple of God ever who came to the rescue & said "God; I will do whatever you ask". God spoke and said, "Joe, you will be hated by many when your murder that child". "I know" said Joe, "but many will gather together in prayer, thus, raising the vibration of the entire planet". God asked again, "Are you sure"? Joe replied "anything for you God", as he descended back to Earth to fulfill his blueprint for life. When Joe became a man, he did indeed take the life of that small child. Imprisoned for his crime he suffered the rest of his life in remorse. Many hated him; repulsed by his actions, even questioning God by asking "why, was this done"! Most are still unable to understand the full picture. Some are unable to understand that not only had Joe chosen that life; but that little girl selected to die exactly in that way before she was born. It is truth; when hearing of these horrific acts; every human became consumed in compassion. In such massive compassion; Earth obtained an enormous shift, a healing that would not have otherwise occurred.

We ask you this day to embrace everyone with love. Can you look your enemy in the eye and say "I Love you"? Knowing he is of the same breath as you. One with all Creation.

Bless you my children. You have embraced the path to enlightenment and we are proud to be guiding you.

We love you. Jesus Christ and the Legion of Angels

Greetings Dear ones. I Am Hilarion, Ascended Master and Chohan of the 5th Ray of Truth, Science, Vision, Healing and Prosperity. I am the Master Healer of the Universe. One of my incarnations was St. Paul (Saul) at the time when Jesus Christ walked the earth. During such times of terrible health issues in the world today, you may call upon me for healing. It is reccomended that you begin with a prayer, connecting to God, and through God, you may call on me. At such time, you will see/ feel/ hear or imagine something unique to our connection. It is this, that will solidify our connection. For example, when you call on me, if you smell apple pie, then that smell is our link. If you are to see a candle in your minds eye, then that candle is our link. If you imagine the warmth of a cuddly teddy bear, that so shall it be. Our Link. Our connection. Then from that time forward, when you acknowledge our connection, it will be that connection you can use to call upon me, at any time thereafter. At times of ill feelings, call upon me, tell me in your words exactly what you are feeling, thinking, seeing and of course, smelling... use all of your earthly five senses. Then, quietly rest. Give me time to access your situation and adjust it as necessary to bring you back into balance and wholeness once again. Normally this takes approximately one half of your earthly hours. At the end of this time, you may ask me questions, or give me an update on your status. When you ask a question, the very first idea that comes into your mind will be the answer to your question... This is how I will speak to you. Slowly at first to solidify our connection and for you to get used to this process. In subsequent times it may be much longer; as you need. I am here for you now and always. All you have to do is call upon me. Until such time; follow the earthly measures. Make sure nutrition is adequate to keep your body strong.

Blessings to all, Love to all, Hilarion

Greetings Dear Children of the Light,

You have asked; What is the significance of a Portal? When we speak of a portal, it is the alignment of such properties of not only the planets, the Stars, the Moon and the Sun. It is also an alignment of the Universal & Galactic energies in such a way as to produce an opportunity for certain magnificent energies to be available for use not only for your-self but for your entire planet. In Prayer, gather and absorb these energies. Focus them for the highest good of your-self, for like it has been said while in a commercial airplane... "place the oxygen mask on yourself before helping anyone else" We are sure you can recall this phrase if you have ever traveled through the air. This is true. For if you are not at peak awareness, health and courage then you will not be able to help another. Focus these energies to raise your own vibration first. Then, use them to help others only after you check with your highest guidance; if it is in your best interest to help at that time. For there is a fine line between enabling and disabling. Remember one story in the Bible; "teach a man to fish"... then he eats for a lifetime? If you feed him fish... then he can only rely on you.

Many years ago when our Host Elizabeth first learned Reiki, she wanted to Fix everyone; thinking she can heal the world. We recall her saying "No one needs to be in pain ever again!" What a long, hard lesson it was. We are happy to say she finally realized that each person had signed up for many lessons in this lifetime. Some actually need that pain for their own Soul to succeed.

Before removing anyone's lesson for them, (for if you did; you would take on their Karma!) you should connect with God/ your Higher Self, and ask the three most important questions of healing. Can I, May I, Should I??? Can I = do I have the ability to do this? May I= do I have permission from God/ the Universe? And Should I = is it in MY highest and best interest??? If you do not receive a positive "YES" for all three of these questions; STOP. Send a Prayer, and let God do the rest.

Yes, there are actually times when it is not your business. Yes, there are actually times when it is best for you to say a Prayer, and only "Hold Space" as your Shamanic Teachers taught. Yes, there are times when you will hold a client's head in your hands, and God will take over, not even letting you understand what is happening because the healing is between God and the Client and NOT you. Honor the Sacredness of the Healing work and being a Clear Conduit for God. This is the true meaning of the words Clear Clean Conduit for the Energy work. When you channel the energy from God to the Client with Unconditional Love in your heart, you become a Clean, Clear Vessel for God's Light & Love to flow through you to the Client. Amazing energetic shifts can take place during such time. You call them miracles.

During the Portal Opening we advise you to absorb and digest these wonderful energetic gifts. They will not only raise your consciousness, but will raise each individual vibration in each human wishing to partake. Go forth in Love and Light, Oryon.

Ancient Wisdom

is the crème of the crop of

Spiritual Wisdom gathered

during fourteen years of study

with Spiritual Masters

from all over the

world and

beyond…

www.ancientwiz.com